WOMEN IN SCIENCE

Rachel Carson

*Marine Biologist and Winner of
the National Book Award*

Cavendish
Square

New York

Meghan Rock

Published in 2017 by Cavendish Square Publishing, LLC
243 5th Avenue, Suite 136, New York, NY 10016
Copyright © 2017 by Cavendish Square Publishing, LLC

First Edition

CPSIA Compliance Information: Batch #CW17CSQ

All websites were available and accurate when this book was sent to press.

Library of Congress Cataloging-in- Publication Data

Names: Rock, Meghan.
Title: Rachel Carson : marine biologist and winner of the National Book Award / Meghan Rock.
Description: New York : Cavendish Square Publishing, [2017] | Series: Women in science | Includes bibliographical references and index.
Identifiers: LCCN 2016034445 (print) | LCCN 2016037070 (ebook) | ISBN 9781502623195 (library bound) | ISBN 9781502623201 (E-book)
Subjects: LCSH: Carson, Rachel, 1907-1964--Juvenile literature. | Biologists--United States--Biography--Juvenile literature. | Environmentalists--United States--Biography--Juvenile literature. | Women biologists--United States--Biography--Juvenile literature. | Women conservationists--United States--Biography--Juvenile literature. | Carson, Rachel, 1907-1964. Silent spring.
Classification: LCC QH31.C33 R63 2017 (print) | LCC QH31.C33 (ebook) | DDC 570.92 [B] --dc23
LC record available at https://lccn.loc.gov/2016034445

Editorial Director: David McNamara
Editor: Elizabeth Schmermund
Copy Editor: Rebecca Rohan
Associate Art Director: Amy Greenan
Designer: Alan Sliwinski
Production Assistant: Karol Szymczuk
Photo Research: J8 Media

Printed in the United States of America

CONTENTS

Rachel Carson and her microscope.
Her wonder and enjoyment of science
led her to write her many books on
marine biology and the environment.

INTRODUCTION

AN ENVIRONMENTAL PIONEER

Today, the air in the United States is clean enough to breathe safely, and there are strict regulations against water pollution. This was not always the case. The main reason for this, and for the environmental movement in the United States, can be traced back to a talented writer from Pennsylvania. Rachel Carson, born in 1907, worked as a government scientist for most of her career. However, it is not her work as a government employee, but rather her career as a science writer that she is best known for today.

Rachel Carson's most famous book, *Silent Spring,* came out in 1962, and it took the world by storm. Carson, who spent four years carefully researching and writing the book, presented a damning case against the **chemical** DDT, which is short for **dichlorodiphenyltrichloroethane.**, DDT is a powerful insecticide. During World War II, it was used to protect troops from insects carrying diseases like malaria to great effect. When the war ended, chemical companies began to promote DDT as a wonder compound. By applying it to crops, farmers could get rid of common pests and increase crop yield. The US government used it broadly to try and eradicate pests like the fire ant and the gypsy moth. Unfortunately, these applications proceeded with almost no research into its potential environmental effects. And there was growing evidence that DDT also significantly impacted birds, other wildlife, and even humans—not just insects.

This is where Rachel Carson stepped in. After her first three books were released to critical acclaim, she became well known and respected. Next, Carson set out to write about the effects of insecticides like DDT in *Silent Spring*. The book involved careful research into a variety of fields, but particularly **ecology** and **toxicology**. Ecology is the study of interactions between **organisms** and their environment. As a science, ecology was just gaining acceptance when Carson began her work on *Silent Spring*. One of the main points she emphasized in all her books was the interconnected nature of the world. One cannot affect one part of the **ecosystem** and not cause effects somewhere else, which are often unforeseen due to the complex nature of the natural world. The other science that played an integral role in her book was toxicology, the study of the effects of toxins on organisms. At the time, toxicologists typically studied the catastrophic effects of fatally large doses of chemicals. In *Silent Spring*, Carson wrote about the impacts of non-lethal exposure on a long-term timescale, leading to a change in how toxicology is performed today.

Today, Carson is known as a pioneer of the environmental movement, and her impact is hard to measure because it is so vast and powerful. *Silent Spring* nurtured a grassroots environmental revolution that swept the world. Thanks to her, the effects of chemicals are more carefully considered, with environmental protection regulations at a federal level in most nations. While there are still challenges facing the world today in regard to chemical use and its impact on people and the environment, the world is a better place because of Rachel Carson and her work.

The Carson family farmhouse, now named the Rachel Carson Farmstead, has been preserved as a historical site and museum.

CHAPTER ONE

EARLY LIFE AND EDUCATION

Rachel Carson became an influential marine biologist and ecologist, but she started off life like many other children of her time. Throughout the course of her young life, she would develop an interest in reading and writing, as well as nature, and see the world change around her at the dawn of the twentieth century.

THE CARSON FAMILY

Rachel Carson was born May 27, 1907, in Springdale, Pennsylvania. Her parents could not know at the time that she would go on to change the world. To Robert and Maria Carson, she was their youngest daughter and a welcome addition to the family.

Maria Carson was a retired schoolteacher. She doted on her youngest child and spent many hours walking around the family's property with her and reading books to her. For much of Carson's life, her mother was her closest confidante and trusted friend. It is possible that she made sure her daughter could do whatever she wanted because of her own lack of options as a young woman and her abandoned teaching career. Her father, Robert Carson, struggled much of his life to find his place in the world. He worked off and on as a salesman, a worker at the local power plant, and a clerk. His health often kept him from working long or hard hours, and he had a hard time holding down any one job, which meant that he struggled to provide for his family. The Carsons often squeaked by with enough, but they did not have any significant financial means.

The Carsons' two older children, Marion and Robert Jr., were both less scholastic than Carson. Her siblings often struggled to find their place in the world. For her sister Marion, this led to a rash marriage and trying to leave the family home several times when she lacked the means to support herself. Her brother also suffered from an unhappy marriage. Both siblings moved in and out of wherever the family home happened to be throughout their lives.

LIFELONG INTERESTS

Because Rachel Carson was often on her own as a child, books and the wilderness around her offered companionship. It was in the early years of Carson's life that her love of nature and reading blossomed. When she was in grade school, she began writing her own stories. Without many children her age around the farm where her parents lived, much of Carson's free time as a child was spent with her mother exploring the family's property or reading books. Her mother was very interested in a philosophy of children's education that promoted teaching children about the natural world as a way to explore religion, morality, and other important topics. Because of this, Maria often took Rachel on

BEATRIX POTTER AND
PETER RABBIT

Rachel Carson cites Beatrix Potter as one of her favorite writers from childhood. The influence Potter had on Carson is particularly obvious in Carson's earliest writings from childhood starring animal protagonists. Potter was responsible for writing thirty books over her lifetime. Most popular were her stories about animals, like *The Tale of Peter Rabbit*. Potter also had a lesser-known passion for scientific illustration and painting. For her paintings and studies of mushrooms, she was particularly well respected among mycologists (scientists who study fungi). At the time, however, Potter was not able to go to school and study science to further this interest.

Over the course of her life, Potter would also become an important conservationist in England. With money from her book sales and an inheritance from a family member, Potter bought a piece of property in the Lake District (an area in the picturesque northern countryside of England). For the rest of her life, she progressively bought more and more of the properties around her home to preserve the countryside from development. Potter's land became the basis for the Lake District National Park. Today her work is still celebrated and read throughout the world, much like the work of the woman she would inspire—Rachel Carson.

long walks and fostered her daughter's interest in the natural world around them.

Maria also encouraged her youngest daughter to read. As a young girl, some of Carson's favorite books were Beatrix Potter's books, particularly *The Tale of Peter Rabbit*, and Kenneth Grahame's *The Wind in the Willows*. With her interest in reading, it did not take long before Carson was writing stories of her own. Her earliest pieces often showed her love for and understanding of nature, as well as the influence of writers like Potter and Grahame on her. But her first published story was inspired by her brother's service in WWI; titled "A Battle in the Clouds," it was printed in *St. Nicholas* magazine. Carson would join the ranks of other illustrious writers whose first works appeared in the pages of *St. Nicholas,* including William Faulkner, F. Scott Fitzgerald, and E.B. White. Over the next several years, she would publish several more stories in the magazine, including her first piece of nature writing, a story about her and her dog going on a walk and looking for birds on their property.

EDUCATION

Carson's elementary school education was spotty. Her mother often kept her home when there were outbreaks of illness. At the time, many of the diseases going around were fatal. In 1918, for example, the Spanish flu pandemic would kill an estimated fifty to one hundred million people over the course of a year worldwide. Unfortunately, many childhood diseases proved fatal, and Maria Carson was unwilling to risk her youngest daughter's life.

In spite of her spotty attendance, Carson was able to keep up with her classmates. Between her intelligence and diligence and her mother's past as a schoolteacher, Carson was rarely behind in school. When it was time for high school, the family was at a crossroads. The local school only went

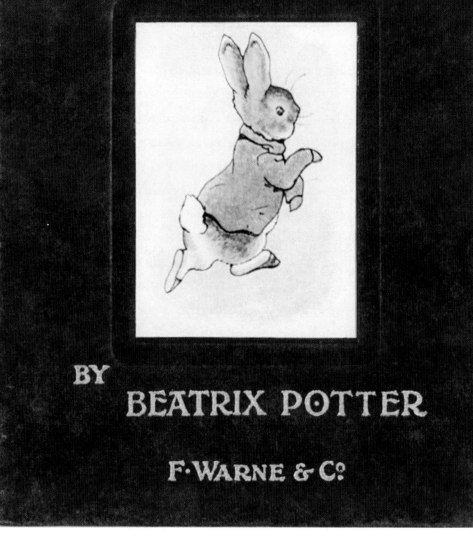

THE TALE OF PETER RABBIT

BY BEATRIX POTTER

F·WARNE & C.º

Books like The Tale of Peter Rabbit *had a huge impact on young Carson and helped foster her love of nature.*

to the tenth grade, but the closest four-year school would cost too much in transportation to attend for four years. So they compromised. Carson attended the local school for the first two years to save on trolley fare, and then transferred to the four-year Parnassus High School. Parnassus was an excellent fit for Carson. The school was small, and its teachers devoted much to the education of their students. Unlike her siblings, Carson made the decision to attend college and further her education, planning to get a degree in English and pursue a career as a writer.

She was able to get a scholarship to attend Pennsylvania College for Women (PCW). The school was good scholastically but had the added bonus of not being far from her parents' home, so her mother could visit often. Carson started off as an English major and then moved on to biology halfway through her schooling. This was seen as a very unconventional course by many of her fellow students. In one letter to a friend, Carson wrote, "I've changed my major. To what? Biology of course. Miss Skinker hasn't recovered from the shock yet. She says after this nothing will ever surprise her."

After her college career, Carson decided to continue on to get her master's degree at Johns Hopkins University. The family had a difficult time paying for her graduate school and was already struggling to make payments on loans for her undergraduate degree. Eventually, her whole family moved to Baltimore so they could be closer to her and share the cost of living. Carson completed her degree in 1932 after some difficulty finding a suitable project for her thesis. She taught **zoology** at Hopkins and was hoping to go on to get her doctorate degree but had to leave school to help support her family when her father died.

MENTORS

Rachel Carson was lucky enough to have two mentors over the course of her life. The first and foremost was her mother, who encouraged her throughout her life and was one of Carson's closest confidantes. Later, in college, she found Mary Skinker, who set her on the path to study biology and follow a career as a government scientist.

Maria Carson

Maria Carson was mother, confidante, and friend to her daughter. Because Carson never married, they would live together almost all of their lives, except for Carson's time in college and briefly in grad school. The relationship between them was extremely close, and at times, others viewed it strangely. The relationship between Maria and Rachel Carson would define both of them. They supported each other, emotionally and financially.

Her mother's encouragement allowed Carson to pursue an unusual career for a woman—as a biologist. Part of her encouragement and expectations may have been driven by Maria trying to live vicariously through Rachel because of her own lackluster marriage and abandoned teaching career. Every weekend when possible, Maria Carson would travel to see her daughter at college, and they would go to the library together and study. Her desire for Carson to only have the best extended not just to her daughter's schooling, but also to the company she kept, one friend of Carson's from college noted.

Mary Skinker

Mary Skinker was a biology teacher at PCW, and a very popular one at that. The youngest daughter of eleven children from a family in St. Louis, Missouri, Skinker was a determined scientist and educator.

Carson in her high school years at Parnassus High School, where she flourished

Rachel Carson: Marine Biologist and Winner of the National Book Award

After obtaining her teaching certificate, she taught college in New York before getting a job at PCW. Skinker was very well liked by her students and extremely popular, in spite of having high expectations from her students.

Skinker was also an excellent biologist and encouraged Carson to pursue a career in science. After many talks with Skinker and her favorite English professors, Carson made the decision to switch to biology as her major. Skinker inspired Carson to continue her studies at Johns Hopkins University, where Skinker was going for her doctoral degree. With her connections to Woods Hole Oceanographic Institute (WHOI), Skinker helped get Carson to the ocean for her studies.

Skinker also encouraged Carson to go to graduate school, although she was honest about her struggles to find employment after leaving PCW. When she successfully obtained a job with the US government, she was adamant that Carson should consider working for the government as a way to make a living as a scientist. Skinker found there were not many opportunities for female biologists as faculty at universities and struggled to find work during the Great Depression.

THE ERA OF HER CHILDHOOD

Carson grew up between two eras marred by the events of a World War. When she was younger, life on the family farm was peaceful and sleepy. As industrialism kickstarted in the United States and progress sprinted forward, the stream by their house would be overrun with pollution and the two power plants in her town would blanket Springdale in dirt and noise. Seeing these changes, particularly when she returned home from college, was jarring for Carson and had a profound impact on her. In addition to what Carson experienced in her early home life, the First World War and the political and social movements of her childhood altered her views, as well as the world she lived in. The burgeoning environmental movement, for instance, had a large impact on her and inspired her own **conservation** work later in life.

World War I

In the earliest part of her childhood, Carson would also see one of the nation's greatest conservationists in office: President Theodore Roosevelt. Theodore Roosevelt would, under the Act for the Preservation of American Antiquities, create bird and game preserves, national forests, and national parks. In total, he is responsible for protecting more than 200 million acres of land.

When she was ten, the United States joined the fight against Germany and entered World War I. Her older brother, Robert Jr., would join this fight, too. Her first published story was actually inspired by imagining her brother fighting the Germans in Europe, though he was stationed in Canada for much of his service. Because she was so young during the war and the United States was only involved for a year, much of the tragedy and devastation of World War I never reached the rural Carson homestead to make an impression on the youngest Carson daughter.

The Roaring Twenties

In the 1920s, Carson's family struggled to stay afloat in spite of more prosperous times for many Americans. For many people in the United States, the twenties were only prosperous for the wealthier members of society. The Carson family only had modest-to-slim financial means, and her father had a hard time keeping a job. Her mother took on piano students for twenty-five cents a lesson.

When she was thirteen, women won the right to vote with the passage of the Nineteenth Amendment. For much of the previous fifty years, women's rights activists had been fighting for suffrage; now that they finally had it, their goals changed. Women's organizations of the time focused on world peace, rights for workers (particularly women and children), and welfare programs. Carson was likely inspired by these female crusaders who so doggedly sought change. Later in her life, she would lead her own campaign for change, starting with her seminal work on pollution and the hazards of **pesticides**, *Silent Spring*.

Starting from her earliest childhood, Carson was passionate about both the natural world and the written word. It was her talent as a writer, as well as her understanding of science, that would allow her to go on and change the world.

Carson's official photograph as a US Fish and Wildlife Service employee.

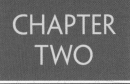

CHAPTER TWO

RACHEL CARSON'S TIMES

achel Carson lived in a time of great change—but she was also a woman who helped change those times herself. Starting in 1900, the United States of America would undergo a radical transformation. There was great social change, but also industrial and economic change. People moved from farms to the city as a new industrial age began. The car became the common mode of transportation, and scientific advances led to many people living better lives through innovations from penicillin to television and computers. In her lifetime, Carson witnessed two world wars, a global depression, the ecological disaster of the Dust Bowl, the rise of the military-industrial complex, and the discovery of the **atomic bomb**. All these experiences impacted her and how she would approach the world around her.

THE HISTORIC AND CULTURAL CONTEXTS OF CARSON'S WORK

Rachel Carson lived and worked in a world experiencing incredible changes. The historical and cultural contexts of her work are almost impossible to separate as the two are so closely intertwined. The United States went from winning a world war to becoming embroiled in a decades-long cold war, the advancement of nuclear weapons put the world on edge and, in the United States, the rise of the civil rights movement and feminism signaled a larger culture of change. Carson's most important work could not have come at a time more rife with changing the status quo, and her work itself was a pivotal part in changing the world around her.

Under the Sea Wind

Carson's first book, *Under the Sea Wind,* examined the lives of animals in the water. Published in 1941, the book sprang from an essay first commissioned by her boss at the **Department of Fisheries** (now the Fisheries and Wildlife Service, or FWS), which was eventually published in *Atlantic Monthly.* The book was not particularly popular by any means, though it received

Carson's older brother was a pilot fighting for the allied forces during World War I, much like these men here.

favorable reviews from critics. Just one month after the book's release, the bombing of Pearl Harbor and the United States's entry into World War II would overshadow Carson's work. Her book sales were mediocre at best, probably due to this shift in national focus. Carson's friends pointed out that the war would eventually end and her book would still be great, but Carson remained discouraged.

World War II and the Cold War

The Second World War was a prolonged military conflict on a global scale. Weapons were more advanced than ever before, and the devastation they wreaked was staggering. All told, between the Holocaust in Europe, the atomic bombings in Japan, and the deaths of soldiers and civilians on both sides, an estimated fifty to eighty-five million people lost their lives during this time. But at the same time, science was hailed as the savior of people on both sides and made huge strides. During the war, the chemical insecticide dichlorodiphenyltrichloroethane (commonly known as DDT) was frequently used to prevent against malaria and typhus. It saved the lives of soldiers as well as citizens in areas where these diseases were prevalent. The advent of the atomic bomb, hailed as a masterpiece of particle physics and chemical engineering, was another example of the terrible advances of science during the war. Even the scientists involved in the **Manhattan Project** (the United States's top-secret group working to develop a nuclear weapon) were awed and horrified by what they had created.

The historic and cultural events of the post–World War II era often centered around the burgeoning cold war between the Soviet Union (USSR), a communist power, and the United States, a capitalist power. These countries battled for dominance in any and all arenas, including sports, science, and politics. At that time, communism was the number-one enemy in America. In their witch-hunt for potential "Commies," Senator McCarthy and the House Committee on Un-American Activities would run roughshod over the country. "Communism" became a four-letter word.

Science was one arena that advanced leaps and bounds in the arms race between the two super powers. The USSR and the United States battled for supremacy over the upper atmosphere with satellites, then manned probes, culminating in landing a man on the moon. Culturally, science was glorified as making these advances possible and seen as a way to beat the Communists at last. You could put your trust in science—it was saving lives and making the world a better place, or so it seemed to many people in the post-war period. This notion of science as savior would last until the late 1950s, when discoveries of the dangerous effects of some of these scientific advances were brought to light.

Nuclear Weapons

A top-secret project was taking place throughout the 1930s and World War II. Thanks to Albert Einstein's work at the turn of the century, and that of many other particle physicists that followed in his wake, scientists realized that an atom could be split. Einstein himself, after renouncing his German citizenship, sent a letter to then-president Franklin Delano Roosevelt (FDR) urging the United States to start research into weaponizing nuclear energy as soon as possible. He felt a nuclear bomb would be possible, and more importantly, that Germany may have already been developing one. Splitting an atom would release a mind-boggling amount of energy. Governments soon realized that this scientific discovery could be turned into a weapon of enormous power, unlike anything ever seen before.

The United States did indeed set out to develop a nuclear weapon. The top-secret effort was called the Manhattan Project, and it involved many of the top physicists of the day. On July 16, 1945, the first successful test of a nuclear bomb occurred at a secret testing ground in New Mexico, near the Los Alamos military base. President Harry Truman, taking over after the death of FDR, finally made the decision to unleash the weapon upon Japan rather than continue what would be a costly and devastating war. The first bomb was unleashed on the population of Hiroshima, Japan, killing 75,000 people and injuring another 100,000 people. When Japan did not surrender, Truman ordered a second bomb dropped on Nagasaki three days later, killing even more Japanese civilians. Thousands more victims eventually died from cancer and other long-term health effects of exposure to radiation from the bomb.

The advent of the nuclear age had begun, and World War II was over at last. The environmental impacts of the nuclear radiation from the atomic bombs would take years to come to light. As the USSR and America entered an arms race, ever more powerful bombs were tested.

The Civil Rights Movement and the Rise of Feminism

But the nuclear arms race was not the only new development changing the world. Starting in the 1950s, there were broad cultural changes happening across the United States. The first of these changes was the beginning of the civil rights movement. Though African Americans in the United States were no longer slaves, in many ways their social condition remained the same. Jim Crow laws kept many African Americans from voting, and they experienced the inequality of segregation. During this time there was also a resurgence in racial violence led by groups like the Ku Klux Klan (KKK). After fighting in two world wars and suffering through the Great Depression, many African Americans had had enough of the status quo. The fifties marked the beginning of a move toward equality for all Americans, regardless of their race.

In 1954, the US Supreme Court ruled in *Brown vs. the Board of Education of Topeka, Kansas* that segregation was unconstitutional and that segregated schools inherently created inequality. Chief Justice Earl Warren wrote, "We conclude that in the field of public education, the doctrine of 'separate but equal' has no place." The court decision would mark the beginning of the modern civil rights movement. More court decisions were handed down on desegregation, and there was tremendous pushback from the white establishment in these areas. In 1955, the civil rights movement received greater media attention due to the brave actions of a woman named Rosa Parks. After a long day of work, Parks refused to stand so a white man could take her seat on the bus. This was against the law, and Parks was arrested for her civil disobedience. These two events would begin a cascade of change and civil disobedience to achieve equality for people of color in the United States. The push for equal rights was not limited to African Americans, however. American Latinos and Native Americans strove to gain equal rights for themselves across the country. Women, too, would raise their voices for more rights that had been restricted due to their gender. Women at the time earned sixty cents for every dollar a man made in a similar job. Feminism and the women's liberation movement sought equal pay, equal rights (many women could not get a credit card without their husband's approval, for instance, even if they had their own jobs), and access to safe and legal family planning methods.

The late fifties and the sixties were defined by a passionate generation of youths tired of the status quo. They wanted equal rights for people of color and women. They believed in the importance and inherent value of the environment. As a whole, American youths questioned the establishment and its values, policies, and belief system. The nation was a melting pot coming to a boil, and the population had never been more volatile or ready for change.

Questioning Science

At the time, there were also several events that led people to begin to question the safety of chemicals and scientific advancements coming out of the Second World War. The first event was the discovery that **thalidomide**, a drug given to expectant mothers for nausea, caused significant birth defects. Children born from thalidomide pregnancies had malformed, shortened limbs, and often had issues such as deafness, blindness, and mental disabilities. This shocked the public and rocked the scientific and medical world. Because of thalidomide, the federal Food and Drug Administration (FDA) raised its standards for drug testing before a compound could be declared safe for human use. The public also began to question the safety of new chemicals and drugs on the market.

The other event that led to a change in public opinion sprang from the nuclear testing that followed World War II and defined the early Cold War period. Strontium-90, a toxic compound that is released during nuclear testing, was found in the milk of dairy cows. Scientists realized that the chemicals released during aboveground nuclear tests did not just stay safely in the upper atmosphere. Rather, they fell to the earth and entered the ecosystem. Strontium-90 landed on grass and hay, which dairy cows then ate and absorbed. They passed along this compound in their milk, which then entered into the homes of Americans. Strontium-90 was not only in the milk of dairy cows—further testing showed that it was actually in the teeth of infants of the time. The public was so concerned about this that the Atomic Energy Commission (developed from the Manhattan Project) hired ecologists to do formal ecological studies detailing the effects of nuclear testing on ecosystems. One area in particular that was studied was in Bikini Atoll, a testing site for the thermonuclear (hydrogen) bomb, a new kind of bomb that was much more powerful than the atomic bombs dropped during World War II. Scientists there discovered that even though the chemical had dissipated from the environment, it stayed in the tissues of the fish and wildlife and was passed from generation to generation.

Both these discoveries led people in the United States and elsewhere to question the safety of things they are exposed to daily and the supposed benefits of scientific advances. The results of the Bikini Atoll studies also led the public to worry about the long-term impacts of exposure to dangerous chemicals, including effects on future generations. The assumptions scientists made when determining whether certain chemicals were safe were based on a false set of conditions. Scientists assumed that Strontium-90 would not enter the ecosystem at large, for instance. These flawed assumptions illustrated the need for further testing. The world's ecosystems, as well as our own bodies, were much more nuanced and complicated than anyone had anticipated. It became clear to many people that one seemingly small chemical could massively impact a system, including the ecosystem as a whole.

Culturally, it is clear that there was a rising discomfort with scientific advances in the late fifties. Many science fiction films of the time depicted monsters created by the effects of nuclear bombs and testing. This was particularly apparent in the cinema of Japan, with films like the Godzilla series about irradiated monsters awoken from the sea by nuclear testing, and in the United States, with films like *Them!* about irradiated ants of giant size. These films may contain ludicrous monsters and special effects, but they represent real cultural fears about the effects of science on the environment and on life itself.

CARSON AND THE WORLD AROUND HER

Rachel Carson was a woman of her times and a woman ahead of her times. She did not just impact the world around her; she was also greatly affected by the events she lived through. The same events that defined her country and her generation had huge impacts on her personal life as well.

The Great Depression

Carson was unlucky enough to graduate from college just a few months before the Great Depression hit the United States and the world. In spite of her family's economic hardship, she managed to continue her graduate studies. She found a position in Raymond Pearl's lab at Johns Hopkins University. Pearl was a major player in the field of ecology and population biology, and Carson learned quite a bit from him. She graduated with her master's degree from Johns Hopkins in 1934 and struggled to figure out what to do next. What she really wanted to do was continue on in graduate school to obtain her PhD. For a few years, she was able to help support her family by teaching zoology at Johns Hopkins. In the end, the decision about further education was made for her by her

Carson observing a specimen at the beach. Going out to explore tide pools remained a favorite activity all her life.

family's dire financial straits. At her friend Skinker's urging, she took the civil service exam and obtained a position in the Department of Fisheries (now the Fisheries and Wildlife Service, or the FWS) under Elmer Higgins. The position could not have come sooner, as shortly thereafter her father died suddenly of a heart attack.

Though she did not know it at the time, her new job would set her on an unforeseen career path. Her first assignment was to write a series of radio scripts about the sea. Several other scientists in the department had tried, but all had failed. They were knowledgeable in their fields but not good at communicating that knowledge to a public audience. Luckily, Carson had been unknowingly preparing herself for this task her whole life. Her love of nature, her talent for writing, and her understanding of science made her the perfect person for the job. When she handed in her first scripts, it was clear she was a fantastic science communicator, and Higgins was bowled over by the quality of her work. It was also the first time that Carson realized her two loves—writing and science—could be combined as a potential career. She quickly became the writer for the department and often helped colleagues revise their papers for publication.

In 1937, her older sister passed away, leaving Carson and her mother caring for her two young nieces. She remained the sole breadwinner for her family, and to help bring in extra money, she began to publish freelance articles with various magazines and newspapers around the area. This brought in extra cash, but it also led to her first book deal to write *Under the Sea Wind*. During this early period, Carson remained somewhat unsure of her work and herself, but the financial situation at home forced her to press on in spite of any doubts. It had the added benefit of honing her skills even further as a writer and communicator.

World War II and the Carson Family

Carson continued to work for the US government throughout the war. Her duties were somewhat minimal and removed from the war efforts for the most part. At home, she volunteered to run an air raid siren. Her one task at work that related to the war effort involved writing a series of pamphlets about eating fish. Due to the shortages of meat, many families were without beef, pork, and chicken. The FWS put out a series of pamphlets written by Carson about the benefits of eating fish as an alternative to meat. Carson started looking for other employment in 1945, at the end of the war, but found that pickings for biologists were slim. She eventually decided to stay on in her position and, in 1949, was promoted to head editor for all FWS publications.

Though she was pleased the war was over, a deep foundation of Carson's belief system was shaken. Before the end of the war, her childhood and experiences of the natural world led her to believe that man was incapable of irreversibly harming the natural world. When the nuclear bomb dropped on Hiroshima, Carson realized that mankind had a tremendous and terrible power to do permanent harm.

Post-War America and Carson's Rise to Fame

In 1948, Carson began to seriously consider leaving her position at FWS and working full-time as a writer. This was a risky proposition, but in the end she felt she would be happier doing this. She hired Marie Rodell as her literary agent, and the two quickly became friends. Rodell was instrumental in getting Carson her next book contract. Her second book, also on the topic of life in the sea, was finally published in 1951. *The Sea Around Us* was an almost instant hit. Her meteoric rise to fame and the praise for her second book took Carson by surprise.

The Sea Around Us was on bestseller lists for eighty-six weeks, and she went on to win the National Book Award and the Burroughs Medal. The success of her book also helped relieve her family's financial worries, which were not insignificant.

The sudden rise to fame, however, could not have come at a worse time for Carson's family. Her niece, Marjorie, who she had cared for since her sister's death in 1937, became pregnant out of wedlock. The scandal this could cause if it became known would have been almost unbearable for the Carson family. Carson did her best to steer away any questions of Marjorie's husband and the sudden addition to her family, but the worry that it would come to light hung like a black cloud over Carson's head. The family drama greatly reduced Carson's ability to enjoy her sudden popularity and the success of her book.

After the success of *The Sea Around Us,* Carson was ready to tackle another book. Her final book in the so-called "sea trilogy" was *The Edge of the Sea.* This time, she focused on the lives of marine creatures on various types of shores. The result, in 1955, was another successful publication. It proved to her critics and her supporters that Carson was not a one-hit wonder. This time was somewhat idyllic for Carson and her family. They were financially secure, Carson was a successful writer and well respected in the literary and scientific worlds, and she had time to focus on future endeavors.

In 1957, her niece Marjorie passed away, leaving her young son, Roger Christie, an orphan. As Carson had for all of her adult life, she stepped up once again. She decided to adopt Roger in spite of the complications of taking on a young son while also caring for her ailing mother. She moved the family from Maine back to Maryland so Roger would have access to better schools. The transition was fraught with emotional turmoil for both her and Roger. In the first months living with his great-aunt and great-great-grandmother, he struggled with being alone and often interrupted Carson while she was trying to work. Tragedy struck again when Maria Carson, whose health had been declining for some time, finally passed away. Roger once again had to deal with the loss of a family member.

In spite of the personal tragedy happening in the Carson family, 1957 also marked a change in Carson's professional focus. Carson began to look toward conservation more specifically and talked about buying a section of land near her cottage in Maine to protect it from development. At the same time, she was also increasingly concerned about the sweeping use of pesticides like DDT and their potential environmental effects. When she worked at FWS, she saw the reports their staff scientists wrote on the effects of DDT and other pesticides on wildlife and knew a broader use of them could be very dangerous. In fact, Carson began calling these pesticides "**biocides**," stating that they affected all kinds of life and not just insects. In 1957, Carson began to closely follow reports of government plans to eradicate the fire ant and gypsy moth by spraying this chemical.

During the process of researching and writing *Silent Spring*, Carson struggled with her own ill health. She was finally diagnosed with breast cancer and, though she had a radical mastectomy to remove the tumor, the cancer eventually spread throughout her body. In spite of this, Carson continued to work as much as she could. Though she worried that she would succumb to her illness before she could finish, Carson pushed through to complete the book in 1963. When she received the first comments back from her editor on the completed manuscript, Carson felt a surge of joy. She stated, "All last night the thoughts of all the birds and other creatures and all the loveliness that is in nature

THE GYPSY MOTHS OF LONG ISLAND AND THE BIRTH OF SILENT SPRING

Marjorie Spock and Rachel Carson first struck up a correspondence when Spock became involved in a trial against the government for DDT spraying in Long Island, New York. While some argue that Carson was not interested in DDT until Spock's letters, the evidence is clear that she was concerned about the pesticide from as far back as her time at FWS. Spock was an avid fan of Carson's work and encouraged her to tackle the subject of DDT's dangers in a book. At first, Carson was reluctant and contacted other authors (like E. B. White, who wrote *Charlotte's Web* and was a noted conservationist himself) about writing a book on the subject. All these efforts were for naught, and Carson finally realized she was the only one with the knowledge, experience, and talent to bring the book to life.

Her response to the widespread use of DDT was to tackle it in the same way she tackled many other problems: through research and writing. At first, her editors were not interested in the book subject and worried about the bottom line of publishing such a book. However, Carson and Rodell managed to interest the editor of the *New Yorker* as well as the chief editor at Houghton Mifflin in the project and it got the go-ahead.

The gypsy moth was the subject of an intense eradication program led by the US government.

came to me with such a surge of deep happiness, that now I *had* done what I could—I had been able to complete it—now it had its own life."

EXPECTATIONS AND OPPORTUNITIES FOR WOMEN

Many people consider Carson to be a more modern kind of feminist. In a *Life* magazine interview she once said, "I'm not interested in things done by women or by men but in things done by people." Carson was less interested in gender and more in what people could do to change the world for the better. Her colleagues at the **US Fish and Wildlife Service** said it did not matter if you were male or female in her eyes, as long as you got your work done and did it well.

Throughout the course of her life, women struggled toward equality. When Carson was twelve, suffragettes won the right to vote. In the 1920s, as she attended high school and college, she watched the modern woman emerge. There were heretofore unheard-of sexual freedoms for women as a new era took hold. In addition, for the first time, there were more people living in cities than in rural communities in the United States. These new urban women were in the workforce, as well. And in just a few short years, the Great Depression would force anyone who could find a job to work, women and men alike.

During the world wars, three million women would move into the workforce to fill jobs that men left in order to fight. An additional sixteen million women who were already working would switch from their former jobs to jobs supporting the war effort. Their new jobs were often manufacturing positions that were previously held by men and were considered male-dominated roles. A symbol of the importance of these wartime women workers is Rosie the Riveter. "Rosie the Riveter" was first a song and later a painting. The words above her head in the now-famous Westinghouse poster say "We Can Do It!," and it became a symbol of feminism and women in the workforce. Globally, this increased the acceptance of female workers as important members of the workforce, but after both world wars, they were pushed out of the jobs they held so men returning from war could fill them once again.

In post-war America, while women slowly continued moving out of domestic roles and into the workforce. they were often passed over for promotions and paid significantly less than a man would be for similar work. There was a lot of discrimination still, especially in science and academia. This is one reason Carson looked for work in the governmental sector, rather than in academia. There were almost no positions available for female biology professors that were not at all-women colleges.

When she did get her government position, Carson was one of two professional women at Fish and Wildlife in the whole department. Luckily, she had a series of female role models, like her mother and Mary Skinker, to encourage her on her path despite the difficulties she would face. Women at this time rarely made up any significant percentage of positions of power or heads of department. This made her promotion to editor-in-chief for all FWS publications even more impressive. In spite of the challenges of being a female scientist, she was making a successful career for herself.

The advertisements of the time, however, showed that the "ideal" woman was a homemaker devoted to her house and family, queen of the domestic realm. Carson in no way fit this mold. Many people believed that women leaving the house to go to work professionally endangered their children because they would not have a parent always at home. When Carson adopted her great-nephew, this became a concern for her as well, and she struggled as a working single parent.

A young Carson, around twenty-six years old, facing the Great Depression and getting ready to become her family's sole breadwinner.

One advantage Carson experienced as a woman was that she was constantly underestimated by the establishment. When she started working on her research for *Silent Spring,* the chemical companies manufacturing DDT and the government agencies that used DDT heavily did not take her inquiries seriously. They would come to regret this misjudgment of her talent and fortitude. When the book was finally released, it was clear that her being a woman had not made her book lesser in any way.

Later, one of the ways the chemical industry criticized her after the publication of *Silent Spring* was by attacking her through the lens of **misogyny**. Her critics called her a crazy spinster, remarked upon her appearance, and questioned her abilities to even understand science because of her gender. Because she had never married or had children of her own, they questioned why she should even care about the future generations. These attacks may have hurt Carson, but she laughed them off. The sexist attacks were also ineffective because the work Carson had done stood on its own, regardless of her gender.

Carson and her adopted great-nephew often went on forest hikes with his friends, which she used to help teach them about the natural world.

CHAPTER THREE

RACHEL CARSON'S FIELD OF STUDY

Ecology as a science is relatively new. The term itself was only coined in the last two hundred years, in comparison to older fields like biology and physics, which have been studied for thousands of years. Rachel Carson did not refer to herself as an ecologist until one of her last speeches in 1963. This was not uncommon, as many scientists we now consider the founders of modern ecology did not consider themselves ecologists.

In her 1963 speech at the Kaiser Symposium, Carson said, "It is from the viewpoint of an ecologist that I wish to consider our modern problems of pollution." For much of her life, Carson was a marine biologist and writer. But as she aged and saw the devastating effects of man on the natural world she cherished, she realized she must do her part to educate, conserve, and protect the environment. Through her research for *Silent Spring*, she would come to consider herself an ecologist. Today, her legacy in the fields of ecology and environmental science is unquestioned.

FROM MARINE BIOLOGIST TO ECOLOGIST

Rachel Carson started off her career in science as a passionate marine biologist. From her first trip to see the ocean at Woods Hole Oceanographic Institute, she was hooked on the sea. For much of her earlier life, she had read writers who wrote of the sea. Although she did not live close to the water, she imagined what the ocean must look like. Thanks to Mary Skinker, her biology teacher at Pennsylvania College of Women, she finally made a pilgrimage to the water.

When she began work at the Department of Fisheries, Carson worked primarily as a writer and researcher. She would write papers for her colleagues on very different subjects. But Carson was also responsible for writing more broadly for a public audience about the Department of Fisheries' work. This included conservation efforts that they were undertaking as well as ecological studies.

As she worked on *Silent Spring*, ecology became an inherent part of her book. Carson learned that the effects of DDT were not felt by a single organism, but rather by the entire ecosystem. In order to explain this, she had to become much more familiar with the emerging science of ecology as a way to explain why DDT and other pesticides were so harmful.

OVERVIEW OF ECOLOGY

In the 1700s, a scientist named Carl Linnaeus revolutionized the fields of science and biology. Linnaeus's *Systema Naturae,* an impressive piece of research based on his botanical work, popularized binomial nomenclature. Nomenclature refers to a systematic way we create names for the organisms around us. Rather than using a long and complex Latin name that might differ from country to country, Linnaeus proposed that scientists use a generic name that referred to the genus of an organism (a class of similar organisms closely related) combined with a name denoting the specific species. Humans, for instance, are known as *Homo sapiens*. *Homo* is our genus and *sapien* is our specific species. By producing a way to clearly name and catalog different types of life, he promoted the study of ecosystems as a whole and the budding science of ecology.

In 1866, Ernst Haeckel coined the word ecology. He originally spelled it "oecology," which came from the Greek word "oikos" for household and "ology" for study. However, it is not Haeckel but Eugenius Warming who is considered the father of modern ecology. After much work, Warming published his opus, called *Plantesamfund* ("Oecology of Plants"), in 1895. One of the key concepts Warming introduced is how nature solves similar problems in similar ways despite using different raw materials. This was the first book written on ecology, and Warming went on to teach the first university course in the subject, as well. Warming's definition of an ecosystem as a group of organisms living in the same place, interacting with each other and their environment, was also an important concept in ecology. Many modern ecologists of the twentieth century were hugely influenced by Warming's views and work.

The study of ecology is important because of the information it provides us about a system of working organisms. In Carson's time, ecology was still in its relative infancy, and many people did not consider it a "hard science" like physics or biology. But its importance became apparent in Carson's time as scientists struggled to understand the full impact of things like widespread pesticide use, the effects of nuclear bomb testing, and the general effects of rapidly changing landscapes due to human expansion.

Ecology is also tied inexorably with conservation. In many ways, the popularity of ecology grew out of conservationism at the turn of the century. As the industrial revolution took hold, it became obvious to people that the environment was suffering at the hands of humans. This led to a rise in conservation efforts, popularized by President Theodore Roosevelt and his expansion of the national parks system in the United States. Conservationists frequently turned to ecology as a way to base their advocacy in scientific fact. Conservation and ecology are two sides of the same coin: the desire to protect an ecosystem from harm, and the desire to understand that ecosystem and all its parts.

Ecology and evolution are also tied together. When Darwin first proposed evolution by the process of natural selection, he said that changes in an environment are what lead to changes in an organism. When ecologists observe organisms in an environment, it is important that they consider the history of these living things and how that has influenced the environment itself. For instance, when life first began on Earth, the concentration of oxygen in the atmosphere was much lower. It is through living things breathing out oxygen that the atmosphere was drastically changed. And it is the oxygen in the atmosphere that formed the ozone layer, which today protects the planet from the sun's ultraviolet rays. This, in turn, influences how organisms evolve and develop. So the relationship between living things and their environment is not a one-way street, but rather something reciprocal.

As organisms change an environment, future generations of organisms will change in response to those environmental changes. This is how animals develop ecological niches, or special ways they interact with an environment, from how they eat and reproduce to where they live. Charles Darwin's finches from the Galapagos Islands are an example of this. Darwin realized that the birds likely shared a common ancestor, but they changed over time to adapt so they could better eat a particular kind of food. Over many generations, the beaks of the finches changed from a common ancestor's shape to new, distinct shapes adapted to the food sources they ate. As the finches interacted with their environments, they also evolved to their environment. In this way, evolution can be considered a study of ecology and interactions between organisms and their environment on a much longer time scale.

Transfer of Energy

One important ecological concept is the transfer of energy. The goal of all life is to obtain and maintain energy. For plants, this involves using photosynthesis to turn sunlight and carbon dioxide into sugars and oxygen. Organisms that cannot make their own energy from sunlight and carbon dioxide must find external sources of energy from plants or other organisms, taken in as food. This is the basis of the transfer of energy and the interrelationships of organisms in an ecosystem.

In every ecosystem, the base organism that synthesizes sugar and energy from the environment is called the **primary producer**. Organisms are not always plants; they may be algae, and they may not use photosynthesis either. Deep in the ocean at hydrothermal vents, the primary producers are algae that chemosynthesize—meaning they take carbon dioxide and chemical compounds like hydrogen sulfide coming out of the vents to create sugars. Consumers are organisms that cannot make their own energy, and they get their name because they must consume or eat energy rather than make it

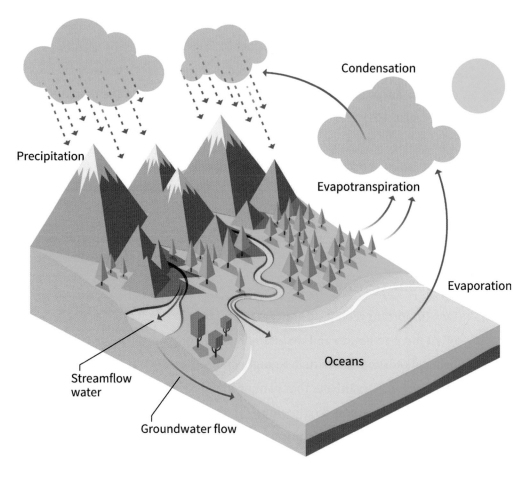

The water cycle allows water to change forms and locations, moving around the globe. Water is one of the most important factors in an ecosystem.

themselves. There are several levels of consumers, called primary, secondary, tertiary, and so on. At the end of the food chain are the organisms responsible for breaking down detritus like dead plants, animal waste, and dead animals. These organisms are responsible for taking waste products from the other **trophic levels** and recycling nutrients back into the soil for plants. Each of these levels of producer and consumer is called a trophic level. All the trophic levels of an ecosystem together form a **trophic pyramid**.

For example, if we consider the ecosystem of a common garden, the primary producers would be the plants in the garden that rely on photosynthesis for their energy. The **primary consumers**, or first level consumers, would be creatures like snails and slugs, birds eating seeds, and mice. If you are an unlucky gardener, you may experience deer and rabbits attacking your plants as well. **Secondary consumers** include animals that eat other animals. These would be creatures like birds, which eat worms or bugs, house cats, which eat birds or mice, and so on. The top-level predator of a garden might be a fox or an owl, capable of consuming secondary level (and sometimes primary level) consumers. In the garden, detritivores are animals like the worms in the soil, the woodlouse (also known as "roly polies") in branches and logs, and mushrooms growing on decaying matter. Altogether, the animals in the garden are an interacting system exchanging energy.

It is important to remember that there is always energy loss in a system. In addition, upper-level consumers are limited by the consumers and producers below them. Since energy is always lost between trophic levels, predators must be scarcer than their prey or face dying out. If there are not fewer predators than prey, there will not be enough prey to sustain them, and only some of these predators will have enough food to survive.

To illustrate the relationships and energy transfer between different consumers and producers, ecologists often use a **food web**. Even seemingly complex food webs do not show all the interactions. This is because an organism rarely eats *only* one thing—specialization of this nature is often very limiting and can lead to extinction. An example of the danger of over-specialization is found in the great panda and koala, both of which have such a specialized diet that they are being driven to extinction from habitat loss and the resulting scarcity of their food sources.

The Water and Carbon Cycles

The world's water supply is an interconnected series of events, almost like a food web. Water molecules travel through the atmosphere as a vapor and eventually form together to create clouds. The winds created by temperature differences in the atmosphere move the clouds, and as the clouds move, they may eventually reach the right conditions to create rainfall. Today, another important part of the **water cycle** is water treatment plants. These were created to clean the water that comes from human establishments. This includes water from human residences as well as for industrial and agricultural uses. Water treatment prevents human pollution (in the form of waste and **synthetic** compounds) from entering the ecosystem and harming organisms.

The **carbon cycle** is similar to the water cycle in the way that carbon is cycled in the world. Because matter cannot be created or destroyed, carbon goes through several different forms but is never destroyed or created. Plants use carbon dioxide and sunlight for photosynthesis, creating sugars for energy. Animals consume plants for sugar and breathe in the oxygen that plants release. Carbon can be found in all life on our planet, as well as in the oceans and atmosphere. This cycle is affected by humans through the burning of **fossil fuels**, such as the use of gas in automobiles. Too much additional carbon dioxide in the atmosphere creates **global climate change**.

Scientific Methods of Ecology

Early criticism of ecology as a hard science revolved around its perceived lack of clear scientific method and analysis. But at the turn of the century, several scientists developed new techniques and mathematical models to explore and expand ecology. The quantitative analysis and experimental methods of ecology that developed at this time included population study and sampling methods.

In the twentieth century, ecologists also began studying populations by marking, trapping, and taking samplings. While it would be impossible (or at least very time consuming and expensive) to capture *every* bird in a forest, scientists can put up special nets in areas and catch a sample of those birds. When scientists do this, they have to be sure the nets are installed correctly and there's no bias in where they have placed them (for instance, an area where they will catch both young, old, male, and female birds). From this, scientists can then figure out what the population is like from the statistical models and the information they have from the birds they did catch.

Of course, sampling with nets will work for some things, but not adult plants or more sedentary organisms. For this, ecologists use the quadrat. Frederic Clements was a plant ecologist specializing in plant succession, or how different plants grow and change in an area over time. He developed the quadrat as a way to perform his studies more scientifically. The quadrat is a square of determined size that is laid on the ground. Then ecologists will catalog all the organisms in that square. To get a scientific sampling, they will do this several times (usually at least three quadrats and often more than ten) and then look at the population distribution of what they observed in all the quadrats they cataloged. Ecologists may also have several quadrats that they study over a period of time to look at **community** changes in population and distribution. Today, the quadrat is still used by ecologists because of its ease of use, functionality, and repeatability.

THE BUILDING BLOCKS OF *SILENT SPRING*

It was only in the twentieth century that ecology developed as a "big science," meaning that it began to be viewed, like physics, chemistry, and biology, as a hard science. In order to develop as a big science, ecologists developed scientific ways of experimentation and ways to confirm ecological hypotheses. But there were struggles between different versions or applications of ecology from the beginning.

Public Concerns

In the early post-war years, many Americans believed in the progress of science and the benefits of man-made compounds. If Rachel Carson set out to publish *Silent Spring* ten years earlier, it is likely her book would never have become a best seller, and she would have been written off by the vast majority of Americans. However, in the late 1950s, two things turned the tide of public opinion and made people begin to question compounds that they were told were benign. The first was the result of the nuclear age and the atomic cold war. The second was a compound believed to be safe that proved disastrous for thousands of newborn infants.

In his book *Nature's Economy: A History of Ecological Ideas*, Donald Worster writes, "The age of ecology opened on the New Mexican desert, near the town of Alamagordo, on July 16, 1945, with a dazzling fireball of light and a swelling mushroom cloud of radioactive gases."

As the immense destructive power of the nuclear bomb became known, many of the scientists of the world worried for what would come. J. Robert Oppenheimer, head of the Manhattan Project, recited a line from the *Bhagavad Gita* immediately after the successful nuclear test: "I am become Death, the shatterer of worlds." Oppenheimer and other physicists of the day grew very worried about what the world would become in the advent of the nuclear bomb.

In this new atomic age, many were shocked and horrified by the destructive powers of the atomic bomb. It was worrisome on an environmental, political, and scientific basis. For Carson herself, she questioned the benefit of man controlling such a power. Not only that, she and several other scientists in the burgeoning field of ecology worried about the environment and the devastation that followed nuclear bombing and testing. And on a political level, seeing the nuclear arms race across the globe harkened to a scary reality: it would only take one match to set off the nuclear powder keg. In spite of the dangers of nuclear bombs, aboveground testing continued.

In 1958, nuclear testing was halted when a series of multimegaton hydrogen bombs caused dangerous amounts of radiation in the atmosphere. But the radiation did not stay in the atmosphere—it fell to the earth in rain and entered the food chain. A study by the Committee for Nuclear Information at Washington University revealed the presence of Strontium-90 in babies' teeth. The next year, *Consumer Reports* released a study showing that Strontium-90 was detectable in cow's milk. By 1960, the nation was gripped by fears of nuclear fallout and the dangers of the previous decade of testing. Under the mushroom cloud of atomic testing, the new movement of environmentalism would begin to form. In an effort to restrain the use of science to dominate nature, environmentalism used the insights of ecology to back up its advocacy.

The other event that had a major impact on public opinion regarding chemicals was the discovery of the dangers of a compound called thalidomide. Thalidomide was a drug that was prescribed for sedation and sleeplessness and was supposedly safe. But, starting in the summer of 1961, Canada and Western Europe had a startling rise in the number of children born with phocomelia, a rare condition. Phocomelia led to deformed limbs and organs, particularly showing in the foreshortening of the arms and legs, with hands and feet very near the torso. It did not take long for scientists and doctors to realize these cases were related to the use of thalidomide by pregnant mothers. Of the 10,000 cases of thalidomide-related phocomelia in newborns, only half of the infants would survive due to life-threatening deformities of the heart and lungs. While thalidomide was apparently safe for non-pregnant people, it led to a public outcry and major concern over the safety of many chemicals and drugs.

Paul Brooks, editor-in-chief at Houghton Muffin, realized that the time was ripe to publish *Silent Spring*. Concern about the scientific advancements of the recent age meant that the public would be willing to listen to Carson's warnings about widespread pesticide use. Brooks wrote to Carson about the fears of nuclear fallout:

《《 *The parallel between effects of chemicals and effects of radiation is so dramatic that people can't help getting the idea. In a sense, all the publicity about fallout gives you a head start in awakening people to the dangers of chemicals.* **》》**

Carson herself followed the results of thalidomide testing. As the first excerpts of *Silent Spring* were published, concerns about thalidomide appeared frequently in the press. Just two weeks before the publication of *Silent Spring*, one journalist from the *New York Post* asked Carson about thalidomide. "It is all of a piece, thalidomide and pesticides—they represent our willingness to rush ahead and use something new without knowing what the results are going to be," Carson responded. Like the public, she was making the connection between modern scientific developments and the potential harm that could come from them without careful study and consideration.

Scientific Studies of the Time

For Rachel Carson's work to be thorough enough to withstand the chemical industry's inevitable criticism, she would need to draw from a variety of resources in a variety of scientific fields. To do this, Carson would turn to the latest ecological and toxicological studies.

Ecological studies of pesticide use formed the basis of her book. In particular, Carson wrote about the way that pesticides bioaccumulate in the food chain. As energy moved up the food chain and became concentrated in larger and larger consumers so, too, would pesticide concentrations grow. This, scientists realized, was how the pesticide even at low concentrations had such devastating effects on organisms higher up in the food chain.

Toxicologists of the time began switching their focus from compounds like arsenic to looking at the effects of new synthetic chemicals. Toxicology is the study of poisonous compounds to life, in particular for humans. *Silent Spring* would have been impossible without toxicologists like Morton Biskind. The most important part of new toxicology was also the study of environmental toxicology, which looked at the effects of chemicals on a whole ecosystem. Many people were involved in this new cross-disciplinary field, including scientists George Wallace, Joseph Hickey, and Frank Egler.

EUGENE ODOM ON ECOLOGY

The book *Fundamentals of Ecology*, written by Eugene Odum, would change the world of ecology. Odom was writing his textbook at an important time for their science and the world at large. As the public began to question the morality of the new scientific advancements and the cost of progress, the field of ecology would be called upon to answer important questions about the natural world. In *Fundamentals of Ecology*, he wrote:

> Until recently, ecologists were content to describe how nature "looks" (sometimes by means of fantastic terms!) and to speculate on what she might have looked like in the past or may look like in the future. Now, an equal emphasis is being placed on what nature "does," and rightly so, because the changing face of nature can never be understood unless her metabolism is also studied. This change in approach brings the small organisms into perspective with the large, and encourages the use of experimental methods to supplement the analytic. It is evident that so long as a purely descriptive viewpoint is maintained, there is very little in common between such structurally diverse organisms as spermatophytes [plants with seeds], vertebrates, and bacteria. In real life, however, all these are intimately linked functionally in ecological systems, according to well-defined laws. Thus the only kind of general ecology is that which I call a "functional ecology," and this kind is of the greatest interest to all students of the subject, regardless of present or future specializations.

Nuclear fallout experiments ordered by the Commission on Nuclear Energy also advanced ecology quite a bit. In particular, one of the first major ecological studies on the effects of radiation was performed in the Marshall Islands in the area that the US military was testing nuclear and thermonuclear bombs. They found that environmental radiation dissipated fairly quickly. However, when they began to study the effects of radiation on the food chain, they discovered that for many years after the end of testing, the radiation was still there after five years in the fatty tissues of the animals of the area. In turn, the radiation was absorbed into the fatty tissues of any other creatures that ate these tainted organisms, including humans.

DEVELOPMENTS IN ECOLOGY DURING RACHEL CARSON'S TIME

Rachel Carson was very much influenced by the ecologists of her time. Many radical new notions came around as she was working at the Department of Fisheries, and even more so as she began to write *Silent Spring.* For instance, Edward Suess and Vladimir Vernadsky presented the notion of the **biosphere.** They proposed that all the systems of nature were interconnected: ecology, lithosphere, hydrosphere, geosphere, and atmosphere. The more scientists study any one of these fields, the more they seem to find connections in unexpected ways between them.

The Commission on Nuclear Energy also played a major part in the development of ecology as a science. The government wanted to know what the biological and environmental impact of nuclear testing actually entailed. This government funding led to major advances in the science and elevated it in prestige. Two of the major

The Enola Gay, *landing after dropping a nuclear bomb on Hiroshima, Japan. Nuclear fallout created many unforeseen ecological consequences, which helped lead to the acceptance of ecology as a hard science.*

leaders of ecology in the twentieth century would actually have their scientific endeavors heavily supported by various proponents of the nuclear field. The brothers Eugene and Howard Odum worked on various projects studying the ecological effects of nuclear testing and radiation. They were invited along with several other ecologists to study sites around the Marshall Islands, including Bikini Atoll, where the thermonuclear bomb test occurred. With this elevation of government support, the science gained funding, which has always been a hurdle for scientists in burgeoning fields. In addition, the funding allowed the Odums and other scientists to engage in experiments on broad ecological concepts in a remote and ideal laboratory.

Eugene and Howard Odum would go from their experiences in Bikini Atoll back to the United States. Eugene Odum was an ecologist who went on to write the first modern ecology textbook with coauthor Gary Barrett, *Fundamentals of Ecology*. Odum was a champion of Arthur Tansley's ecosystem definition. Arthur Tansley, another ecologist of note, first proposed the term "ecosystem" and was heavily influenced by the science and theories of Eugene Warming. Tansey defined an ecosystem as a community of living organisms and nonliving components making an interacting system together. His work was heavily theoretical, and he had a great impact on mathematical modeling, population dynamics, and ecosystem energetics. Rachel Carson herself strongly agreed with Odum's definition of an ecosystem and championed a similar version in *Silent Spring*. Eugene Odum's specialties were population dynamics and ecological energistics, and he is considered one of the fathers of modern theoretical ecology. The equations of a model provide a mathematical and scientific basis for theoretical ecology. Odum would do more work of a similar nature when the Savannah River atomic weapons plant was built. He was given funds to set up long-term monitoring and a field station nearby. He worked on the marshes, tidal estuaries, and fields of the surrounding area. For Eugene Odum, the idea of an ecosystem included more than just the biology of an area and he would carry this principle of Tansley's into his book. The *Fundamentals of Ecology* was the first modern textbook on ecology, and it defined the new field in many ways as well as teaching a new generation of ecologists.

Though Carson was very ill from her cancer at the time, the interview she did for the CBS special on Silent Spring helped launch the ecological movement around the world.

CHAPTER FOUR

CONTEMPORARIES, CRITICISMS, AND CONTROVERSIES

Rachel Carson's *Silent Spring* was a revolutionary book. And revolutions rarely involve just one person. Carson interviewed dozens of people and read hundreds of articles and reports to write her book. She spoke to doctors, government officials, chemists, entomologists, ecologists, and many others to bring her work to fruition. It makes sense then, that the people she would collaborate with and refer to are not, for the most part, ecologists. Like the study of ecology itself, her book crossed disciplines, and she delved into everything from cancer research to chemistry to **entomology**.

A variety of researchers inspired Rachel Carson's work. She was inspired by her colleagues in the government and their early work on the effects of pesticides on wildlife and humans. As the chief editor for all publications at Fish and Wildlife, any research publications or reports that were going to be distributed crossed her desk. In this way, she was educated early on to the dangers of DDT, though it would take almost a decade before she was ready to tackle the subject herself.

CARSON'S COLLABORATORS

Carson consulted many people, including both scholars and non-scholars. She used an ever-widening web of sources for *Silent Spring*. Luckily, many of the people she worked with in the government were willing to help her get rare reports, and Carson's name opened other doors because people knew her from her earlier work on the so-called **"Sea Trilogy."**

Marjorie Spock

Marjorie Spock was an articulate and intelligent woman, the younger sister of the renowned pediatrician Benjamin Spock, and a writer, educator, and biodynamic gardener. Spock's help and contacts were crucial to Carson. She and Carson met because Spock was a plaintiff in a court case involving the spraying of DDT. Spock complained when the local government of Long Island, New York, began widespread spraying with DDT in an effort to end the perceived gypsy moth epidemic. When the spraying did not stop in spite of her complaints, Spock brought a lawsuit against the government along with eleven other plaintiffs. The case was widely followed but ultimately rejected, and all appeals were exhausted (though it did reach the Supreme Court before being dismissed). Though they did not win the case, Spock and the other plaintiffs did win the right for citizens to file an injunction against the government to halt any potentially dangerous or harmful environmental activity until a full scientific review of the proposed action was completed. This case and its legal decision were two of the events that helped develop the burgeoning environmental movement.

Spock and Carson formed a close friendship through regular correspondence, and Spock became an important link to many other scientists looking at the dangers of DDT. She did everything in her power to help Carson write her new book on the dangers of DDT, including introducing Carson to the expert witnesses called in the Long Island case against government DDT spraying. She diligently collected information from any source she could for Carson's manuscript, including news articles and research from contacts and government reports. She sent her collected sources regularly to Carson for her research and encouraged Carson when the writing was slow or difficult.

Clarence Cottam

Born in 1899 in St. George, Utah, Clarence Cottam went on to earn a bachelor's degree and a graduate degree in biology. He joined the US Bureau of Biological Survey (which was later combined with the Bureau of Fisheries to become the Fish and Wildlife Service) in 1929 as a junior biologist, but he moved around in various government departments that dealt with biological research for the next few years. Eventually, he landed a position in the Division of Wildlife Research as an assistant director, where he stayed from 1946 through 1954. Carson and Cottam had a friendship from their time together in government work, and she respected his work with Elmer Higgins, her boss at the Department of Fisheries. After Cottam retired from government service, he eventually became director of the Welder Wildlife Foundation in Sinton, Texas. This posting gave him national prestige and prominence in the conservation community, and he was able to make recommendations for wildlife policymaking.

Together with Higgins, Cottam wrote about the effects of pesticide use, in particular DDT, as early as 1946. He was alarmed by the effects of the government efforts to eradicate the fire ant

The Baird Ornithological Club, at its 108th meeting. Clarence Cottam, who helped Carson research her book, is seated one in on the right hand side of the photograph.

in his area of Texas, particularly the impact on the wildlife of the area. When Carson contacted him for help on her book, he responded in a letter:

> ❝ *I hope you include both insecticides, herbicides, rodenticides, and fungicides. The whole gamut of poisons should be considered, and I know of no one who is more able to summarize this situation than you. I am sure you will render a great public service.* ❞

The two scientists worked together frequently throughout the writing of the book and enjoyed a lively correspondence. Cottam would review several chapters of the book for Carson, giving additional sources and information, and offering phrasing changes where necessary. During one of his final reviews of her work, he wrote ten pages of edits and comments. With the intense scrutiny and attack he felt the book would come under, he often made notes to include references for her facts or asked her to qualify her opinion. In the letter accompanying his notes, he wrote:

> ❝ *Your writing is superb ... yet, I want to warn you that I am convinced you are going to be subjected to ridicule and condemnation by a few. Facts will not stand in the way of some confirmed pest control workers and those who are receiving subsidies from pesticides manufacturers.* ❞

His comments would prove prescient and his advice invaluable. When the final piece was published, Cottam's advice and recommendations of further sources would help the book stand up to the attacks of Carson's opponents. In 1961, Cottam received the Audubon Medal for his "achievement in the field of conservation and environmental protection." Just two years later, Carson would be awarded the same honor for her work on *Silent Spring*.

Harold Peters

Harold Peters was an invaluable contact and collaborator on *Silent Spring* for Carson. He was with the USDA's Bureau of Entomology and later worked at Fish and Wildlife as a biologist. He was a passionate **ornithologist** and bird watcher in his spare time and had connections in academia and the government, as well as with regular bird-watching organizations across the country. He left Fish and Wildlife in 1949 to work for the National Audubon Society as a research biologist. This work mostly involved traveling around the country and collecting data about the fire ant eradication program and other pesticide programs the US government was spearheading at the time.

The work that made him indispensable to Carson, however, was his intimate knowledge of government spraying programs and their effects. This included the confirmed number of wildlife losses, the components and percentages of different chemical sprays and their use in different areas, USDA harassment of Fish and Wildlife agents, and the suppression of data reported by Fish and Wildlife researchers. As Linda Lear writes in her biography of Carson, "His information was accurate, his sources reliable, and his contacts absolutely invaluable." Without Peters, Carson would have been hard-pressed to find the exact information she needed.

Their friendship and correspondence were invigorating for them both, and the gregarious Peters often wrote chatty letters that contained information Carson not only needed but would be unlikely to find elsewhere. Peters also spoke often of Frank Egler, a man he felt understood the damaging effects of pesticides and was familiar with the uphill battle Carson would be waging with her book.

Frank Egler

Frank Egler was a well-known plant ecologist who was already familiar with the struggles of fighting the government. He spent much of his career trying to get the government to stop the widespread spraying of herbicides alongside popular roadways. Egler searched for alternative methods of controlling plants on the side of roads. Like many other ecologists of his age, and like Carson herself, he was deeply impacted by the experiments on Bikini Atoll and the effect of heavy chemical assaults on the wildlife there. Egler was also alarmed by the frequent use of herbicides to control vegetation and their impact on the environment.

Egler urged the ecologists of the time to study both applied ecology and theoretical ecology equally, and to study human-impacted areas and not just pristine natural environments as was the trend. Like some of the other scientists in the Ecologist's Union (later the Nature Conservancy), he wanted his fellow ecologists to speak up more in the public debate about environmental efforts. His efforts to encourage and foster change in ecology as a science were not tremendously successful. He was so frustrated by this work and the general view of ecology at the time, that when Carson first contacted him for her book he no longer even called himself an ecologist.

Exchanging letters with Carson reinvigorated his enthusiasm for ecology and encouraged him to pick up his work again. When Carson sent the chapter "Earth's Green Mantle" to him for review, he responded with twelve single-spaced pages of comments, notes, and edits. Egler was so impressed with her grasp of the science, the thoroughness of her work, and the exactness of her prose that he would have done anything to help. Carson responded to his very helpful edits in a letter:

Frank Egler was a very important resource for Carson as she wrote Silent Spring. *Working with Carson re-energized him to continue studying ecology.*

Rachel Carson: Marine Biologist and Winner of the National Book Award

Carson would receive similar levels of help from many of the people she contacted for *Silent Spring*. She often made such a positive impression on people that they were willing to go above and beyond. More than that, many of the scientists she worked with realized the great importance of her book and what it would do for the world at large. They also realized that, due to its subject, it would need to be as impervious to critique as possible. Like Cottam, Egler knew that both Carson and her book would be subjected to intense levels of scrutiny and criticism. He did his best to prepare her and the manuscript to weather the storm that would hit when it was published.

George Wallace

An ornithologist at Michigan State University, George Wallace first noticed a serious decline in the robins on campus. Around the area at that time there was also widespread spraying of DDT in an attempt to control Dutch Elm Disease, which is caused by a fungus carried on an elm bark beetle. Wallace was inspired to study the effects of pesticides, particularly on bird reproduction.

Wallace and his students found that when the trees were sprayed to kill the beetles, the pesticide did not quickly degrade. It stayed on the leaves, which then fell to the ground in fall and were composted by earthworms. The earthworms then ingested and stored small amounts of DDT in their own systems. Wallace found that while the DDT was only in minute concentrations within the earthworms, a songbird like a robin eating a dozen worms a day quickly accumulated the pesticide in their own tissues. He realized that it would be necessary for ecologists to find alternative methods of pest control if they were to save the songbirds of the world.

Carson and Wallace maintained an exchange of letters throughout her work on *Silent Spring.* She relied on him for a chapter on the effects of DDT on birds especially and appreciated his efforts in editing for accuracy and clarity. His work with the dead and dying birds on the MSU campus was a terrifying case study on DDT's devastating effects. It was easy for Wallace and his colleagues to tell which birds were poisoned by DDT even before they got back to the lab—the tremors the birds suffered were an obvious giveaway.

Edward Knipling

Edward Knipling was chief of the USDA's Entomology Research Branch. He quickly became interested in the challenges of dealing with pesticide resistance in insects and finding new biological methods of pest control. In mosquitos, for instance, it only took a handful of females to survive DDT spraying and pass on their genes to the next generation—because the breeding cycle was so fast, mosquitos developed resistance to DDT quite quickly.

Carson met Knipling several times and went to his lab to meet with him and see his experiments. After seeing his work and laboratory, she became convinced that with more money funding projects like his, alternative methods of pest control could be found readily. Carson was particularly impressed by insect sterilization experiments on screwworm flies, which caused dangerous lesions on cattle in particular.

Edward Knipling, best known for his technique to sterilize insects, was a helpful resource for Carson when she was writing about alternative pest control methods.

In the sterile insect technique, male insects were sterilized by exposure to small amounts of targeted radiation and released into the wild. There, the sterile males would compete to mate with the fertile males. When they won the competition to mate, the females' eggs would remain unfertilized. Over successive years and multiple releases of sterilized males, populations of unwanted insects could be reduced quite well without any pesticide spraying or other deleterious effects on the environment. Carson was right to be impressed by Knipling's work. Knipling and his collaborator Raymond C. Bushland eventually went on to win the 1992 World Food Prize in recognition for their work on the sterile insect technique.

Morton Biskind

Morton Biskind was a legend and a scientific outcast. Biskind started his career as a toxicologist and nutritionist. By the time Carson was writing, Biskind was retired, but he had already made an enemy of the large chemical companies. It was in 1942 that Biskind first made the connection between exposure to DDT and the ailments he was seeing in his patients, as well as in livestock and wildlife in the area. He focused his research on synthetic chemicals and their effects on human enzyme systems, particularly in relation to cancer. Biskind was an expert on industrial contaminants and human cancer, but that did not make his opinions heard. The medical community viewed him with suspicion due to the unpopular results of his research. And after he gave damaging testimony at a congressional hearing for the Pure Food and Drug Act, Biskind was relentlessly harassed by the chemical industry as well. In 1949, he and another colleague, Dr. Irving Bieber, wrote an article titled "DDT Poisoning: A New Syndrome With Neuropsychiatric Manifestations," which linked DDT exposure to higher rates of polio. In the article they wrote, "Facts are stubborn, and refusal to accept them does not avoid their inexorable effects—the tragic consequences are now upon us." Biskind was subject to ruthless personal attacks as his critics tried to find fault with him and his research. Like Cottam and Egler, Biskind worried for Carson and her world-changing book, having already experienced the phenomenon of scientific notoriety himself.

Biskind was what Carson could have been if she had tried to publish *Silent Spring* in the forties. Fortunately, fifteen years later, the time was right for the world to hear about the effects of DDT. Biskind was happy to lend Carson his support and engaged in highly technical correspondence with her over cellular metabolism and the impact of pesticides on humans. He was another scientist who was engaged by her mannerisms and intelligence, and who put as much work into her manuscript as he could in the editing stage. His reviews were thorough and precise and went far beyond any expectation Carson had when she asked for his help.

Bette Haney

Owing to poor health and Carson's struggles to manage a truly impressive amount of research, the book would have been impossible to complete without her two research assistants. Over the course of research for *Silent Spring*, she would hire two different women to help her with typing, scholarly article synthesis, and the general business of research.

Haney and Carson, in particular, shared many interests. Bette Haney was a senior at Bryn Mawr College studying biology who had already won a science writing prize. They both loved literature, were excellent biology students, and loved research. Haney's job was to review the articles that Carson was interested in (they had a weekly meeting on Monday to go over the articles Carson wanted covered that week), and Haney would read and recap the articles for her. They were an excellent work team and even after Haney applied to graduate school, she came back to help finish the project when the deadline was nearing.

Malcolm Hargraves

Malcolm Hargraves was a **hematologist**, someone who studies blood and disorders of the blood, at the Mayo Clinic. His specialty was the effect of chemical exposure on disorders of the blood, particularly leukemia. His work was controversial in his time, and his results, like Biskind's, were unpopular. Unlike Biskind, Hargraves was generally well respected by his peers, though a few did not trust him because of his willingness to give expert testimony and his participation in public health debates. When Carson wrote to him, he was generous with both his own research as well as the names and documented cases of patients suffering from the effects of pesticide exposure, including their symptoms and diagnoses. The letters between the two encouraged Carson and invigorated her research, as she felt that she was building an ever-greater body of evidence for her work on DDT and its effects. She wrote to Paul Brooks, editor-in-chief at Houghton Mifflin, telling him about a new chapter she was developing on cancer hazards related to pesticides:

“ *To tell the truth in the beginning I felt the link between pesticides and cancer was tenuous and at best circumstantial; now I feel it is very strong indeed. This is partly because I feel I shall be able to suggest the* *actual mechanism by which these things transform a normal cell into a cancer cell … I feel that a lot of isolated pieces of the jigsaw puzzle have suddenly fallen into place. It has not, to my knowledge, been brought together by anyone else, and I think it will make my case very strong indeed.* "

Carson was correct, her synthesis of all the different sciences and the already published research would be both new to the public and damaging to the chemical industry. As a result of Carson's relationship with Hargraves and Cottam, both government critics and opponents of the widespread spraying of pesticides, her access to the USDA Agricultural Research Service (ARS) was restricted. Though some government researchers were untroubled by her interest in their insect eradication programs, the powers that be were clearly growing nervous. Luckily, Carson had friends in the government and was able to complete her research, through sources like Harold Peters and others. Like a dog with a bone, Carson would not give up her quest no matter the obstacles before her, and especially not when she could tell she was getting somewhere.

CARSON'S OPPONENTS

By and large, Rachel Carson's biggest opponents came out of the chemical industry or in some way made their living from it. She was attacked because of her gender and often denigrated through the use of such terms as "spinster" and "homely-looking" (neither of which, of course, have anything to do with her science). Carson, though, was a perfect author for *Silent Spring* since her character was very difficult to attack. She was unmarried, but time and time again she had taken care of her family from her ailing mother, to her nieces, to her grand-

Considered by many the father of modern toxicology, Paracelsus was a major influence on one of Carson's biggest opponents, Wayland Hayes.

nephew. Carson also had an excellent track record as a government employee and was well liked by her former colleagues. And because she was wealthy from her earlier books, she was beholden to no organization or interest groups. Between her career and her personal life, critics had a hard time attacking her. And *Silent Spring* was even harder to attack, though her critics tried.

In the end, though, her work was validated again and again. She herself found it easier to brush off the critics that commented on her marriage status or looks. The debate was clinched for many people in the American public when CBS aired a special hour-long program on *Silent Spring*. They brought in Carson, one of her main critics, and government staff from all levels. It was here that Carson came across as calm, cool, and collected. Linda Lear, in her biography of Carson, writes, "It would have been a masterful performance even if there had been no one else to compare her to, but in juxtaposition to the wild-eyed, loud-voiced Dr. Robert White-Stevens in a white lab coat, Carson appeared anything but the hysterical alarmist that her critics contended." Carson's tireless efforts, and those of her sources and colleagues, created a work that was almost untouchable.

Robert White-Stevens

One of Carson's most formidable opponents was the assistant director of the Agricultural Research Division of American Cyanamid, Dr. Robert White-Stevens. A proponent of synthetic pesticides and their benefits, White-Stevens made a terrific debate opponent. He was fast, funny, and very articulate. In 1962, he made twenty-eight speeches against

THE LIFE OF WAYLAND HAYES

Dr. Wayland Hayes was born in Virginia on April 29, 1917. Hayes was well credentialed as both a PhD and an MD. Hayes himself often looked for inspiration from Paracelsus, considered the father of modern toxicology. Hayes encouraged toxicological and medical research and embodied the spirit of Paracelsus, who wrote, "wherever I went I eagerly and diligently investigated and sought after the tested and reliable arts of medicine." Paracelsus was revolutionary because he made observations directly about nature, rather than relying solely upon ancient texts. And, like Paracelsus, Hayes was skeptical of scientific dogma and determined to make his own observations. Later in his career, Hayes championed toxicology as the answer to the controversy over the use of pesticides. He wrote several books on various chemicals and their toxicology to humans that are still referenced today.

Silent Spring alone. He became one of the industry's foremost critics of Carson and her work.

However, when it came to the CBS program, he did not make a good impression. White-Stevens made the argument against Carson that, "If man were to follow the teachings of Miss Carson, we would return to the Dark Ages, and the insects and diseases and vermin would once again inherit the earth." It was hyperbolic and untrue. In her book, Carson had never said that DDT and other pesticides should be banned, and in addition she carefully presented alternative methods of pest control. Overall, he did not impress viewers in the same way that Carson and her calm, collected, and matter-of-fact manner did. A friend wrote in a letter to Carson after the show aired: "You were superb on the television broadcast, and how delightful that Dr. White-Stevens looked so fiendish!"

Wayland Hayes

Wayland Hayes was the chief toxicologist of the US Public Health Service. One of his experiments that was much-cited in defense of the safety of DDT involved fifty-one volunteers he fed DDT to in their meals. As Carson noted in her research,

❝ *One of my delights in the book will be to take apart Dr. Wayland Hayes's much cited feeding experiment on '51' volunteers. It was '51' for only the first day of the experiment; thereafter the experimentees rapidly lost their taste for DDT and drifted away until only a mere handful finished the course of poisoned meals.* ❞

Carson also disapproved of Hayes's lack of follow-up on the people he had exposed to DDT. As she had found in her research, the effects of the chemical sometimes took years to become apparent, not a few months. She decided to cut the study from *Silent Spring*, but it made a lasting impression on her. The paper Hayes published continued to be used by the government as justification for the safety of DDT, no matter how flawed it was.

Hayes often had favorable things to say about the chemicals he studied as a toxicologist, and he was well liked and oft cited by the chemical industry. In 1954, he wrote, "The health benefits from the use of agricultural chemicals should always be kept in mind in considering the potential hazards involved in the use of these chemicals." He further went on to suggest that when people were poisoned by these chemicals, it was their own fault for improper use or application. In 1961, he wrote derisively about people reading antipesticide articles and attributing their own various medical problems to pesticides. The problem, according to Hayes, was people's imagined sicknesses, not the chemicals themselves. Hayes was also on the CBS program as an expert but did not make an extremely positive or negative impression in the same way Carson and White-Stevens did. Like Carson, eventually he was called before the senate committee that was reviewing environmental hazards, including pesticides. Hayes testified to his belief of the safety of pesticides and synthetic chemicals in front of the committee, but the committee's final findings agreed with Carson and *Silent Spring*.

SILENT SPRING

Silent Spring was a book published at the right time, written by the right author, and it had a riveted audience. When US Secretary of the Interior Stewart Udall dedicated a new lab for the US Fish and Wildlife Service specifically for the expansion of pesticide research, he commended Carson's work. She wrote in a letter to Udall after his speech,

> **❝** *During the years I worked on* Silent Spring, *there were times when I wondered whether the effort was worthwhile—whether the warning would be heeded enough to change the situation in any way. Of course I have been amazed and delighted by the many developments, but I can truthfully say that nothing has pleased me more than the tribute you paid.* **❞**

This would be a common theme for Carson in the time after *Silent Spring*'s publication—overwhelmed by praise for her work and quietly (and enormously) satisfied that her labors were indeed changing the world around her.

Carson near her home: bird watching, reading, and writing.

RACHEL CARSON'S IMPACT AND LEGACY

R achel Carson is a name synonymous today with environmental change, ecology, toxicology, **marine biology**, and literature. She was a pioneer, and her talent for writing changed the world. As the renowned ecologist E. O. Wilson writes in the afterword to *Silent Spring*, "We are still poisoning the air and water and eroding the biosphere, albeit less so than if Rachel Carson had not written." This is true. Her work was pivotal in establishing new legislation and government organizations, but many point out that there are still huge environmental issues to tackle.

THE SEA TRILOGY AND *SILENT SPRING*

While she did research for the government and was a marine biologist in her own right, Carson is best known for her written works. *Under the Sea Wind, The Sea Around Us,* and *The Edge of the Sea* were published between 1941 and 1955. Her first book was well received by her peers but did not sell much. This was mostly in part due to Pearl Harbor and America going to war.

Her second book, however, made her a household name. After the disappointment of her first book, Carson was unprepared for fame and fortune. The book stayed on the bestseller lists for eighty-six weeks, which was almost unheard of for a book on a scientific subject. Around this time, Carson began thinking about leaving government service and pursuing writing full time. She was contracted to write another book about the sea, this time about life on the shores, and that book was also very popular.

At the end of the 1950s, Carson turned her eye to a much larger problem. With her fame bolstering her, she decided to begin work on a project about DDT and its detrimental effects on the environment. This was not a small effort. Carson was familiar with the reports coming out of Fish and Wildlife when she worked there and knew of scientists who were deeply ridiculed for experiments showing the dangers of DDT, like Morton Biskind. Carson devoted herself to the task anyway, and the book became a landmark in the field.

Silent Spring is the book that helped change America in the sixties. Its impact on American society was likened by many to the impact of Harriet Beecher Stowe's novel *Uncle Tom's Cabin.* That book inflamed the debate over slavery in the nineteenth century, while Carson's inflamed the debate over the environment and the widespread use of man-made chemicals in it. *Silent Spring* remains a seminal work on ecology, environmental rights, toxicology, and medical research. What makes it so impressive is not only the thoroughness and accuracy of her science, but the readability and poetry she weaves through it. Today, people still refer to it as a historical success in consumer advocacy and environmental activism.

CARSON'S IMPACT ON THE WORLD

It is hard to talk about Rachel Carson and her impact on the world without also talking about the use of DDT. Because of Carson's book, DDT was banned for nonmalarial uses by most developed countries. Though the chemical companies tried to deny her claims and questioned her credentials, government committees and scientific advisory boards all agreed with her research and conclusions. Some of her proponents argue that Carson's work in limiting the use of DDT has made the chemical itself more effective against insects by slowing the evolution of pesticide resistance.

For many, Carson's greatest legacy is helping foster and jump-start the environmental movement in the US as well as abroad. The **Environmental Protection Agency** (EPA) credits its existence to Rachel Carson and *Silent Spring*. Her work was instrumental in bringing about change and regulation to the environment. She wrote well and cared about her subject. Carson, by the end of writing her book, understood the subject better and on a broader scale than many of the original researchers she worked with. In the same way that DDT affects the body at a cellular level and these effects accumulate and magnify as they go up the food chain, *Silent Spring* started a grassroots movement that lead to legislation like the Clean Air and Clean Water Acts. Government agencies began to realize that DDT and other chemicals they had long been fierce proponents of were destroying the environment they sought to protect. David Browner, a prominent conservationist, said of Carson, "She did her homework, she minded her English, and she cared."

Perhaps most importantly is her lasting impact on the psyche of America. If you bring up *Silent Spring* today, more than fifty years

*The logo of the US Environmental Protection Agency today. The EPA is a
direct result of* Silent Spring *and the environmental movement in the US.*

after its original publication date, it is still well known. Carson
inspired a generation of scientists, ecologists, and conservationists.
Her works stand the test of time, and this means we still read and
reflect on her writings today. The impact of her work is hard to

Rachel Carson: Marine Biologist and Winner of the National Book Award

measure because of the broadness of its scope and the radical changes that it led to in how we as humans think of ourselves and our place in the world.

AWARDS AND ACCOLADES

In 1951, the US National Book Award was awarded to Carson for *The Sea Around Us.* This was particularly prestigious because the award is not often given to works of nonfiction. The presenter for the award said about the book, "It is a work of scientific accuracy presented with poetic imagination and such clarity of style and originality of approach as to win and hold every reader's attention." Carson was flattered by the award and realized how popular her work was becoming. Readers enjoyed the science of the ocean but also appreciated her writing style and lyrical prose. *The Sea Around Us* made her a household name. The National Book Award boosted book sales as well, and for the first time since her father died, Carson could breathe more easily about the family's finances.

As much as she appreciated the National Book Award and the fame it granted her, the prize that Carson most wanted was the Burroughs Medal for nature writing. Established in honor of John Burroughs, an American essayist and conservationist, Carson coveted the award. In 1952, Carson achieved her goal. In her acceptance speech, she began to show some of the convictions that would come to fruition in *Silent Spring*:

> *Mankind has gone very far into an artificial world of his own creation. He has sought to insulate himself, in his cities of steel and concrete, from the realities of earth and water and the growing seed. Intoxicated with a sense of*

his own power, he seems to be going farther and farther
into more experiments for the destruction of himself and
his world. 〞

Carson was already working on her next book of the Sea Trilogy at this time, but her speech shows her shifting view of mankind and his relationship with the natural world.

Her magnum opus *Silent Spring* was published in 1962. The furor that accompanied it was also matched by the praise and accolades she received. For this work, she became the first female winner of the Audubon Medal in 1963. Carson received the medal for her work in conservation—just a year after publication, it was already apparent that her work would change the fate of wildlife for the better.

The greatest honor that Carson received was one she could scarcely have dreamed of: in 1963 (and in the same week she was presented the Audubon Medal), she was inducted into the American Academy of Arts and Letters. Not only was this a lifetime membership, it was also unusual for women to join the group at the time. With only fifty seats when Carson was inducted, there were just three other women sitting at the table. When Carson reflected on the distinction, she said it was "the most deeply satisfying thing that has ever happened in the honors department." At the luncheon to induct her, she was compared to Galileo and Buffon, great scientists and writers. Lew Mumford, president of the academy, said in his introduction, "[S]he has used her scientific insight and moral feeling to quicken our consciousness of living nature and alert us to the calamitous possibility that our shortsighted technological conquests might destroy the very source of our being."

But one of Carson's most important honors was awarded after her death. In 1980, President Jimmy Carter bestowed the Presidential Medal of Freedom upon Rachel Carson **posthumously,** the highest honor a civilian of the United States can receive. Roger Christie, the great-nephew she adopted, went to receive the medal in her stead. President Carter said it eloquently and simply when he awarded the medal:

> *A biologist with a gentle, clear voice, she welcomed her audiences to her love of the sea, while with an equally clear determined voice she warned Americans of the dangers human beings themselves pose for their own environment. Always concerned, always eloquent, she created a tide of environmental consciousness that has not ebbed.*

President Carter was right. Even sixteen years after her death, Carson's work was still making waves and inspiring change.

CARSON AND *SILENT SPRING* TODAY

For many environmental science and ecology students, *Silent Spring* is still required reading. With her work, Carson brought rise to an entire grassroots environmental movement and singlehandedly launched the debate on pesticide use to the center stage of American politics.

In E. O. Wilson's afterword to *Silent Spring*, he wrote that the book itself was still exceptional and worthy of attention because "it marks an important moment in history." Like *Uncle Tom's Cabin* and *Our National Parks,* books that changed our nation, *Silent Spring* raises important questions for Americans both in Carson's time and today.

RACHEL CARSON, NATIONAL BOOK AWARD WINNER

Rachel Carson received the National Book Award on January 27, 1952. The honor was unexpected—it was somewhat unusual for the award to go to a nonfiction book, let alone a book about science. Carson commented on this in her speech:

> [T]his notion that "science" is something that belongs in a separate compartment of its own, apart from everyday life, is one that I should like to challenge. We live in a scientific age; yet we assume that knowledge of science is the prerogative of only a small number of human beings, isolated and priest-like in their laboratories. This is not true. The materials of science are the materials of life itself.

When her first book was published, Carson agreed that the authorship would read "R. L. Carson" because everyone felt that readers would be more likely to take a book on science seriously if it appeared to be written by a man. To have her second book be so well received in spite of her gender was huge. Carson was also pleased that so many had commented on the style of her writing and its poetic nature.

Wilson wrote, "The examples and arguments it contains are timeless lessons of the kind we need to reexamine. They are also timely, because the battle Rachel Carson helped to lead on behalf of the environment is far from won." This is true. Many scientists today point out that pollution, climate change, and a mass extinction all loom over the environment today. However, Carson's work inspires scientists and passionate citizens to keep fighting the good fight. To conclude the afterword of *Silent Spring*, Wilson wrote:

> **❝** *We are still poisoning the air and water and eroding the biosphere, albeit less so than if Rachel Carson had not written. Today we understand better than ever why we must press the effort to save the environment all the way home, true to the mind and spirit of the valiant author of* Silent Spring. **❞**

For authors, too, *Silent Spring* is an important example of understandable technical writing and consumer advocacy. Carson's knowledge of her audience and respect for their intelligence is one of the reasons the book has stood the test of time. She left out the more technical jargon, but still explained the concepts, processes, and implications of the research on DDT. On top of that, her writing is lyrical and poetic. The result is an understandable and compelling piece of literature.

MADE POSSIBLE BY *SILENT SPRING*

Today, the Environmental Protection Agency has the difficult task of regulating environmental pollution and conducting ecological research around the United States. However, the EPA would likely

Carson in 1952 on a research trip with Bob Hines. Her research trips helped her write the sea trilogy and make marine biology approachable for a wide audience.

not exist without Rachel Carson's work. The EPA even cites her as the basis for their organization on their website. Today, it is easy to take for granted the air that is safe to breathe and the water that is safe to drink in the United States. This was not always the case.

In the mid-twentieth century the smog was so bad in some cities that there were air advisories just due to pollution. Because of Carson's work, the US government would go on to sign two of the most important pieces of environmental legislation. The Clean Air Act was signed into law in 1963 and the Clean Water Act became law in 1972. These laws set up standards for what is considered "clean" but also provide penalties for those found to be polluting the environment. They also show a shift in the view of Americans. Before *Silent Spring*, the issue of environmental pollution was not particularly prominent and, more importantly, many Americans did not view the access to clean air and water as basic civil rights. After Carson's work, many more people considered access to an environment free of pollutants a basic human right, and environmental legislation changed to show this.

The result of *Silent Spring* and the ensuing uproar led to the banning of DDT for almost all applications. Many today in the chemical industry criticize the work of Carson and her whistleblowing as an overreaction. Critics of Carson argued that her science was unsupported. Both a congressional hearing and a presidential report easily refute this and agree with Carson's conclusions. Proponents of DDT use argue that limiting its use harms human lives. This particular argument for DDT is confusing because it can be so easily refuted. DDT was banned for broad-spectrum use on food crops and within homes, but it has never been banned for use against mosquitos carrying malaria. When it is used for antimalarial purposes, scientists recommend using the minimum amount needed to affect a population of insects. Supporters of the DDT ban argue that limiting the use of DDT actually extends its effectiveness against mosquitos. Studies show that in as few as seven years of DDT application, the chemical is no longer effective. It is hard to truly estimate how many human lives DDT has saved from disease—and how much damage it has caused to us and our environment in the process.

WOMEN SCIENTISTS INSPIRED BY RACHEL CARSON

Being a woman in any of the STEM (science, technology, engineering, and mathematics) fields is not easy. The demographics have changed significantly in some areas, like biology, and stayed mostly male-dominated in others, like computer science. Because Carson was a woman, a biologist and ecologist, and an incredible author, her impact on many female scientists both today and in the past cannot be overstated. Few female

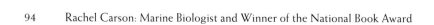

Modern spraying for DDT is very limited and used mostly for malaria prevention. Crop spraying, seen here in Malaysia, is banned in many countries now.

Theo Colborn became famous for her work with endocrine disruption. She was inspired by Carson's work and continued to study synthetic chemicals and their effect on the environment.

ecologists today do not take some form of inspiration from Carson's work and legacy.

Theo Colborn

Theo Colborn, born in 1927, was an avid bird-watcher and had an interest in nature from an early age. After moving to Colorado to become a sheep farmer, she became involved with the Rocky Mountain Biological Station and learned more about ecology and the environment. When she and her husband divorced, she volunteered to do wildlife surveys. Colborn realized that no scientist would take her work seriously unless she had the same credentials as they did.

That is why, at fifty-eight years old, Theo Colborn became Dr. Theo Colborn. When she was in graduate school for her master's degree and doctorate, many of her advisors and professors were uncomfortable around her and unsure of how to treat a graduate student of her age. She was determined and persevered. After her PhD program, Colborn ended up researching the area around the Great Lakes.

When studying the wildlife around the Great Lakes, Colborn found the water relatively clean and free of contaminants, but the animals themselves were still not doing well. As she began to delve deeper into the reasons behind this, she formed the basis of her theory about endocrine-disrupting chemicals. Colborn's report, released in 1988, found that many Great Lakes animals and their offspring suffered from a host of health problems. The list of effects was long and included serious problems like reproductive and immune system complications, behavioral and hormonal changes, altered metabolism, deformities, and tumors. In addition, there was a noted overall population decline in the animals around the Great Lakes. The pollutants affecting the wildlife were known to have similar effects in humans, and though that impact could not be measured in Colborn's first study, it was still considered significant.

Colborn realized the compounds most affecting the wildlife were ones that mimicked natural **hormones** in the **endocrine system,** like estrogen. When the body encounters these chemicals, it treats them like they should be there rather than processing them as something foreign. This causes tremendous problems in most organ systems and results in many of the symptoms the Great Lakes wildlife suffered.

Colborn's work was groundbreaking, but like many of the first researchers looking at DDT, it was confined to the realm of researchers and academics. She wanted to make this problem known to the public at large in the same way Carson had before her. With the help of John Peterson Myers, she published the book *Our Stolen Future.* It was not the immensely popular seller that *Silent Spring* was, but it made waves in academia and industry. Colborn and Myers brought the problem of endocrine disruption to the table for the first time. It also marked a huge shift in the field of modern toxicology. Toxicology traditionally studied the LD-50, or the amount of a chemical it took to create a lethal dose in fifty percent of the subjects in a study. Colborn's toxicology looked at the long-lasting impacts of minute exposure, rather than catastrophic exposure.

To continue her vein of research and encourage others, Colborn founded The Endocrine Disruptor Exchange (TEDX) in 2003 at age seventy-six. She was frustrated with the slow pace of regulation and government and hoped that an organization that supplied credible scientific information would help change the political dialogue.

Colborn was interviewed about Carson's impact on her own science and career on the fiftieth anniversary of *Silent Spring*. Her words show how important Carson's work was for her own: "Carson elevated the consciousness of society about the ravages of man-made chemicals and gave birth to an environmental movement I am sure she never dreamed possible." She greatly admired Carson's work and was impacted by her writing, like many people of the time. "She wanted her readers to think about what the release of untested chemicals can do," Colborn said, "Her message is as fresh today as it was then."

Jane Lubchenco

Jane Lubchenco was born December 4, 1947. Like Carson, she first became seriously interested in marine biology after taking an invertebrate zoology course at Woods Hole Oceanographic Institute on Cape Cod. Her career blossomed from there. She went on to become the first woman appointed head of the National Oceanic and Atmospheric Agency (NOAA) under President Barack Obama.

Lubchenco has also worked heavily in the effects of global climate change on the world's ecosystems and the people living in those ecosystems. She remains hopeful about the situation, though, "I take heart in knowing that social change can happen very rapidly once a tipping point is reached, that young people are bringing new passion and creativity to the issue, and that climate change is being seen increasingly as the moral issue it is."

One of her main impacts today on ecology and conservation is her groundbreaking research in marine protected areas (MPAs). Lubchenco found that creating a no-take zone, or an area where fishing is prohibited but some other forms of human use are allowed,

Dr. Jane Lubchenco was sworn in by Vice President Joe Biden as the first female head of the National Oceanic and Atmospheric Association. Lubchenco herself was inspired by Carson's writing to become a scientist.

improved the health of the animals not just in the zone but around it as well. Lubchenco also established that having a series of MPAs that are close enough to allow animals moving back and forth between them creates a healthier overall ecosystem in a much larger region. Recently, she proposed an effort to have 20 percent of the world's oceans designated as MPAs by 2020 as a way to improve the ocean's health and prevent the dangers of overfishing.

Sarah (Sally) Woodin

Another modern marine ecologist is Dr. Sarah (Sally) Woodin, working at the University of Southern Carolina. *Silent Spring* came out when Woodin was a senior in high school, and her family vacations to the Adirondacks throughout her childhood inspired a love of nature. For Woodin and her family, *Silent Spring* "confirmed what we already had seen in terms of wildlife, the reduction of the dawn chorus [the singing of birds at dawn], the lack of concern for ramifications of treatments. [Carson's] treatise did not come as a surprise." While Woodin was already planning to study science, Carson's work helped her understand intellectually her emotional reaction to nature and inspired her to continue on her career path.

Woodin's work focuses on organisms in the mud and soil, like worms, and how they become "ecosystem engineers." Their normal behavior, like burrowing and creating tunnels, acts to change the environment around them. As the environment changes, it becomes more hospitable for other organisms, and an ecosystem is formed as the site is colonized. Her research methods are novel and include placing microphones in the field to listen for creatures burrowing, and her work is sponsored by organizations like the National Science Foundation (NSF) and NASA. These pioneer organisms that behave as ecosystem architects are also sensitive to global climate change, and a new branch of her research is looking at how global climate change affects the biogeography of ecosystem architects.

Woodin feels that Carson's work is still relevant today for three primary reasons. The first is that the industries that benefit from the destruction of the environment will continue to deny the destruction of the environment. Two, we are still learning. As scientists learn more about fishery sciences, they can help the government make better regulations that protect species more efficiently. And finally, the third reason Carson's work remains relevant, Woodin argues, is that as we make technological advances and discoveries we can "explore new approaches to the world, altering life and interactions in new ways. As we do that there will always be unforeseen or perhaps merely unvoiced ramifications, some good and some terrible." The most important part of all these advancements, Woodin says, is "having people sufficiently brave, erudite, and dedicated to raise those issues that may help us avoid terrible tragedies," like Rachel Carson and E. O. Wilson.

Florence Williams

Florence Williams is a science writer and mother of two. Many reviewers have compared Williams' book, *Breasts: A Natural and Unnatural History,* to Carson's *Silent Spring.* What started her interest in the topic was an article about new research looking into the toxins in breast milk. At the time, Williams was nursing her second daughter and wanted to learn more. In her own breast milk (which she had analyzed at a lab in Germany) they found a higher-than-average amount of flame-retardant chemicals, as well as trace

E. O. WILSON AND CARSON'S WORK

E. O. Wilson, a prominent ecologist today, was one of the first to send Carson data about the fire ant eradication program the United States government was carrying out in the late 1950s. Writing to Carson, he said, "The subject [of DDT] is a vital one and needs to be aired by a writer of your gifts and prestige." Wilson himself is no slouch as a writer or presenter, and he has done much to advance the fields of ecology, environmentalism, and conservationism.

Wilson's particular specialty is in sociobiology (the study of social behavior relative to biology), island biogeography, and biodiversity. This led him to become one of the leading world experts on ant biology and communication. His work in the field of island biogeography led him to better understand the need for biodiversity in an ecosystem as well as conservation to protect at-risk ecosystems.

Wilson has won two Pulitzer Prizes for his books, *On Human Nature* and *The Ants*. In addition to this, he also wrote the afterword for the modern publication of *Silent Spring*. Wilson has been a strong proponent for conservation in the light of global climate change and is a firm believer that we are in another extinction event, like the one that killed the dinosaurs. His eloquence and expertise are both reminiscent of Carson herself, and he is well regarded among his peers and the public as an educator, researcher, and conservationist.

amounts of dioxin, DDT, and a particular jet fuel ingredient. This was startling to her, and she searched for more information.

Williams would go on to perform several small-scale experiments in her own home to determine where the contaminants came from, and how easy it was for her to get rid of them from her body. Her research showed many readers just how common some pollutants and toxins are in one's own home. She writes about how these chemicals, many of them endocrine disruptors, then store themselves in fatty tissues like those of the breast. While many ecologists and scientists have been focused on an external environment, Williams's work focuses on the synthetic chemicals found within our domestic environment and their effects.

Breasts may themselves be considered a kind of "canary in the coal mine" and a warning signal for chemicals accumulating in our bodies. While Carson focused on the effects of synthetic chemicals on birds and wildlife, Williams focuses on the effects of these same chemicals on the human body. Her work is engaging and follows in the path of *Silent Spring* in its groundbreaking nature.

THE NEXT ENVIRONMENTAL FRONTIER

It is hard to talk about the future of ecology and the environment without talking about *Silent Spring* and its impact on the field. The positive impact of Carson's work on both wildlife and humans is undeniable for most scientists. But many ecologists, when talking about Carson's work, bring up the fact that there is still much more to be done to protect the environment from humans today.

The two most major challenges facing us in the modern age are global climate change and the sixth mass extinction. Like

Al Gore, former US Vice President, won the Nobel Peace Prize for his film An Inconvenient Truth, *which discussed global warming and its impacts.*

the use of DDT in Carson's time, these are controversial topics. Today, though almost all scientists agree on the existence of global climate change, politicians and industries that depend on burning fossil fuels fight valiantly to deny its existence. As they once did to Carson herself, they question the science and the credentials of the scientists involved. One key turning point in the fight against this ignorance is former vice president Al Gore's documentary and lecture series, *An Inconvenient Truth*. Like Carson, Gore talked directly to scientists and then boiled down the research and what it means for non-scientists. Today, the environment, but also human lives and livelihoods, are threatened by climate change. As large storms and ecological disasters happen more often and rising water levels affect the planet, politicians and scientists are trying to find solutions. Whether they will succeed remains to be seen.

In Carson's time, animals were dying of DDT and other synthetic chemicals. The same is still true, sadly. Frogs, for instance, are one of the first indicators of a polluted environment because of how easily they absorb toxins through their skin. But the direct reason for the current mass extinction, E. O. Wilson argues, is not just toxins in the environment. It is a combination of toxins, habitat loss, diseases, and climate change that is causing a vast die-off of species diversity. The die-off is also happening more rapidly than any other extinction event on our planet. More than ever, it is becoming clear to ecologists that in order to save species, conservation efforts and reducing pollution will be necessary. This is the only way to stem the rising rate of species extinctions.

These are the ecological challenges facing the world today. They will require changes in our behavior as humans, and a broader appreciation of life on our planet. One of the major themes throughout Carson's books was the fact that all of life is connected. Humans are not alone on Earth, and if we want to keep our planet the way it is, we will have to recognize that and change our behavior. When Rachel Carson accepted the National Book Award, she said in her speech:

« *It seems reasonable to believe—and I do believe— that the more clearly we can focus our attention on the wonders and realities of the universe about us the less taste we shall have for the destruction of our race. Wonder and humility are wholesome emotions, and they do not exist side by side with a lust for destruction.* »

The wholesale destruction of the environment is something that Carson fought against in all her writings and public appearances. Perhaps her greatest legacy is trying to instill in the public a sense of wonder and appreciation for nature. Carson believed that sparking love of the natural world would create change. Carson's work influenced people on a grassroots level to start an environmental revolution while simultaneously changing the minds of policy makers and politicians.

CHRONOLOGY

1907   Rachel Carson is born.

1914   World War I breaks out in Europe.

1917   The United States joins the war in Europe.

1918   *St. Nicholas* magazine publishes Carson's first story, "A Battle in the Clouds"; Spanish flu pandemic breaks out, killing 50-100 million people worldwide by the spring of 1919.

1919   The Treaty of Versailles signals the end of World War I.

1920   Women win the right to vote; Prohibition is established in the United States.

1925   Carson graduates from high school.

1928   Penicillin is discovered.

1929   Carson graduates from Pennsylvania College for Women in May.

1929   On October 29, the stock market crashes, marking the start of the Great Depression.

1931   A ten-year drought begins in the central United States, deepening the Great Depression for many.

1932	Carson gets her master's degree from Johns Hopkins University; physicists split the atom.
1933	Prohibition is repealed in the United States.
1936	Carson is hired by the Bureau of Fisheries as a junior biologist.
1937	*Atlantic Monthly* accepts "The World of Waters," based off of a piece Carson wrote for her job in the Bureau of Fisheries.
1939	World War II begins in Europe.
1941	Carson's first book, *Under the Sea Wind*, is published; on December 7, the Japanese bomb Pearl Harbor and the United States enters World War II.
1945	The United States drops atomic bombs on Hiroshima and Nagasaki in Japan; World War II ends in treaties.
1951	Carson's second book, *The Sea Around Us*, is published in excerpts in the *New Yorker* and then in its entirety.
1952	Carson is awarded the Burroughs Medal.
1955	Her third book, *The Edge of the Sea*, is published.
1962	Silent Spring appears excerpted in the *New Yorker* in June to much acclaim; the book is published later in September.
1963	Carson appears on CBS in "The Silent Spring of Rachel Carson."

1964   Carson succumbs to cancer.

1970   The Environmental Protection Agency (EPA)
       is established.

1972   Congress passes the Clean Water Act and bans the used of
       DDT in the United States.

1980   President Jimmy Carter posthumously awards Carson the
       Presidential Medal of Freedom.

GLOSSARY

atomic bomb A weapon of extreme power created by splitting the nucleus of an atom; later a hydrogen bomb was developed that was even more powerful than the first atomic bombs created during World War II and dropped on Nagasaki and Hiroshima in Japan.

biocide Rachel Carson's term for "pesticides," referring to the fact that their negative effects are not limited to pests but affect a wide range of organisms.

biosphere The part of the world in which life can exist; living organisms together with their environment

carbon cycle The natural cycling of carbon through life on the planet. While carbon dioxide is a normal part of this cycle through plant and animal respiration cycles, the burning of fossil fuels releases excess carbon dioxide and causes global climate change.

chemical A compound made up of elements on the periodic table. The composition and arrangement of the individual elements creates a particular kind of chemical.

community A group of organisms made up of at least two different species in the same general area and time.

conservation The act of preserving an area or a particular organism, conservationism experienced a surge of popularity at the beginning of the twentieth century and again with the rise of environmentalism.

DDT (dichlorodiphenyltrichloroethane) A synthetic chemical that is a potent insecticide and biocide. Rachel Carson's *Silent Spring* revealed its many negative impacts on wildlife and humans, and today it is banned for almost all applications. It is still permitted for use in prevention of malaria and typhus spread by mosquitos.

Department of Fisheries *See* "US Fish and Wildlife Service."

ecology The study of interactions between organisms and their environment.

ecosystem The interactions of a community of organisms and the nonliving components that make up their environment.

endocrine system An organism's natural system for the creation and regulation of hormones. When organisms absorb synthetic chemicals, they may interrupt or disrupt the organism's natural hormone cycles and cause serious harm.

entomology The study of insects.

Environmental Protection Agency (EPA) The organization responsible for protecting the environment in the United States. It is tasked with environmental research programs as well as law enforcement for legislation like the Clean Air and Water acts.

food web A more complex way of visualizing an ecosystem's trophic levels and predator/prey interactions.

fossil fuels Carbon compounds created from the remains of fossilized organisms that lived millions of years ago. Fossil fuels include coal, oil, and natural gas. The burning of fossil fuels is responsible for global climate change.

global climate change The man-made altering of the global climate. Climate change is created by carbon dioxide emissions from the burning of fossil fuels like oil, coal, and natural gas. This is considered a threat to human life, the global economy, and the entire earth's ecosystem.

hematologist A scientist who studies blood and disorders of the blood.

hormone A chemical in the body responsible for regulating many of the body's functions. Synthetic chemicals that mimic natural hormones like DDT can cause very serious health problems in animals and humans.

Manhattan Project The group of nuclear scientists that was responsible for the United States developing the atomic bomb. This led to the formation of the United States Atomic Energy Commission, and later the Department of Energy.

marine biology The study of organisms living in saltwater, like oceans and seas. This was Rachel Carson's scientific specialty.

misogyny A hatred of women.

organism A living being, it can be an animal or plant.

ornithologist A person who studies the branch of zoology dealing with birds.

pesticide A chemical used to kill pests, like insects harmful to crops and humans. Pesticides may be found naturally (many plants contain compounds to deter predation by insects) or can be made by man, like DDT.

posthumously Something that happens after someone's death.

primary consumers The second level of the food chain, these are organisms that survive by consuming primary producers. They are preyed upon by secondary and tertiary consumers.

primary producers The basis of the food chain, a primary producer is an organism like a plant that can create its own food from sunlight and chemicals around it.

secondary consumers The third level of the food chain. These are organisms that prey upon the lower trophic levels.

The Sea Trilogy The first three books Rachel Carson wrote, the second of which made her a national bestseller and author of renown. The trilogy includes *Under the Sea Wind*, *The Sea Around Us*, and *The Edge of the Sea*.

synthetic Something that is man-made and does not occur in nature.

thalidomide A drug prescribed in the 1950s for nausea. It was discovered that pregnant mothers prescribed the drug for morning sickness gave birth to children exhibiting severe mental and physical developmental problems. The connection between the birth defects and the drug was discovered around the time that Carson began to write *Silent Spring*. It led to a change in the national opinion of chemicals and scientific developments.

toxicology The study of the way toxins affect organisms. It is a combination of the studies of medicine, chemistry, and biology.

trophic level The position an organism occupies in the food chain. All the trophic levels of an ecosystem together form a trophic pyramid.

trophic pyramid A way of visualizing the effects of predation and limitation of predators. The base of the pyramid is the largest and forms the basis of the food chain. As trophic levels increase, there are fewer predators, shown by the narrowing of the pyramid.

US Fish and Wildlife Service The department that Rachel Carson worked for as a young staff scientist. She eventually became the chief editor for all publications the department created. Her work in the government gave her the connections she needed later to write *Silent Spring*.

water cycle The natural cycling of water through the atmosphere and in the terrestrial and aquatic environments. Pollution in one area can affect the whole cycle and cause things like acid rain.

zoology The study of life on our planet, in particular living organisms. Botany is its sister group, which is the study of plant life.

FURTHER INFORMATION

BOOKS

Gillam, Scott. *Rachel Carson: Pioneer of Environmentalism*. Edina, MN: ABDO Publications, 2011.

Wadsworth, Ginger. *Rachel Carson, Voice for the Earth*. Minneapolis: Lerner Publications, 1992.

WEBSITES

The Life and Legacy of Rachel Carson

http://www.rachelcarson.org

This website is written by Linda Lear, one of Carson's biographers. It contains concise information about Carson's life and work, as well as information about those she inspired and resources for further information. It has Lear's insight, but is shorter and easier to read than her full biography of Carson, *Rachel Carson: Witness for Nature*.

The Rachel Carson Council

http://rachelcarsoncouncil.org

The Rachel Carson Council is the organization that was established by Carson's friends and colleagues after her death to carry on her work. Today, the website has information about their current programs and information on Carson herself.

VIDEO

Rachel Carson's *Silent Spring* on American Experience

http://www.pbs.org/wgbh/americanexperience/films/ RachelCarsonsSilentSpring

This PBS special for American Experience details Carson's life and the impact of *Silent Spring*.

BIBLIOGRAPHY

Alexander, Carol. *Rachel Carson: Writer and Scientist.* Morristown, NJ: Modern Curriculum Press, 1995.

Ashoka Organization. "What Is Rachel Carson's Legacy? 6 Women Leaders Speak Out on the Message That Still Holds True Today." *Forbes*, October 17, 2012. http://www.forbes.com/sites/ashoka/2012/10/17/what-is-rachel-carsons-legacy-6-women-leaders-speak-out-on-the-message-that-still-holds-true-today/#7b7142dc71ed.

Breton, Mary Joy. *Women Pioneers for the Environment.* Boston: Northeastern University Press, 1998.

Daniel, Pete. *Toxic Drift: Pesticides and Health in the Post-World War II South.* Baton Rouge: Louisiana State University Press in Association with Smithsonian Institution, Washington, DC, 2005.

The Fabulous Century: Hard Times 1930 – 1940. Alexandria, VA: Time-Life Books, 1991.

Foster, John Bellamy, and Brett Clark. "Rachel Carson's Ecological Critique." *Monthly Review*, February 2008. http://monthlyreview.org/2008/02/01/rachel-carsons-ecological-critique/.

Gillam, Scott. *Rachel Carson: Pioneer of Environmentalism.* Edina, MN: ABDO Pub., 2011.

Graham, Frank, Jr. "Rachel Carson." *EPA Journal*. November/
December 1978. https://www.epa.gov/aboutepa/rachel-carson.

Griswold, Eliza. "How 'Silent Spring' Ignited the Environmental
Movement." *New York Times*, September 21, 2012. http://www.
nytimes.com/2012/09/23/magazine/how-silent
-spring-ignited-the-environmental-movement.html.

Grossman, Elizabeth. "Theo Colborn, a Brief Biography." TEDX:The
Endocrine Disruption Exchange. Accessed June 21, 2016. http://
endocrinedisruption.org.

Hudson, David L., Jr. *The Handy American History Answer Book*.
Canton: Visible Ink Press, 2015.

"Just What's Inside Those Breasts." Interview with Florence
Williams by Terry Gross. *NPR*: Author Interviews, May 16,
2012. http://www.npr
.org/2012/05/16/152818798/breasts-bigger-and-more
-vulnerable-to-toxins.

Kinkela, David. *DDT and the American Century: Global Health,
Environmental Politics, and the Pesticide That Changed the
World*. Chapel Hill: University of North Carolina Press, 2011.

Knight, Louise W. *Jane Addams: Spirit in Action*. New York: W.W.
Norton, 2010.

Krieger, Robert I., Ph.D., and John W. Doull, MD, PhD.
"Dedication." *Hayes' Handbook of Pesticide Toxicology* (Third
Edition), December 16, 2009. http://www
.sciencedirect.com/science/article/pii/B9780123743671001427.

Lear, Linda. "Rachel Carson's Biography." Accessed June 04, 2016. http://www.rachelcarson.org.

Lear, Linda J. *Rachel Carson: Witness for Nature*. New York: Henry Holt, 1997.

Lord, M. G. "Unnatural Women." *New York Times*, September 15, 2012. http://www.nytimes.com/2012/09/16/books/review /breasts-by-florence-williams.html.

Mahaffey, James. *Atomic Accidents: A History of Nuclear Meltdowns and Disasters*. New York: Pegasus Books, 2014.

McLaughlin, Dorothy. "Silent Spring Revisited." *PBS*. Accessed June 17, 2016. http://www.pbs.org/wgbh/pages/frontline /shows/nature/disrupt/sspring.html.

Miller, Char. *Gifford Pinchot and the Making of Modern Environmentalism*. Washington, DC: Island Press/Shearwater Books, 2001.

Park, Chris, and Michael Allaby. *Oxford Dictionary of Environment & Conservation*. Second Edition ed. Oxford: Oxford University Press, 2013.

Perrot, Michelle, Francoise Thebaud, and Georges Duby. *A History of Women in the West; Volume 5: Towards a Cultural Identity in the Twentieth Century*. Cambridge: Harvard University, 1994.

Piascik, Andy. "Morton Biskind Warned the World About DDT." *Connecticut History*. Accessed June 15, 2016. http:// connecticuthistory.org/morton-biskind-warned-the-world- about-ddt/.

Pollock, Steve. *Ecology*. New York: DK, 1993.

Popkin, Gabriel. "Why Does Rachel Carson Matter?" *The Sieve*, March 04, 2013. https://the-sieve.com/2013/03/04/why-does -rachel-carson-matter.

Rachel Carson's Silent Spring (American Experience for PBS). Produced by Neil Goodwin. WGBH Boston, 1993. DVD.

Saxon, Wolfgang. "Margaret W. Owings, 85, Defender of Wild Creatures." *New York Times*, January 31, 1999. http://www .nytimes.com/1999/01/31/us/margaret-w-owings-85-defender -of-wild-creatures.html.

"Silent Spring: The Dying Robins of MSU." Michigan State University Museum. Accessed June 16, 2016. http://museum. msu.edu/?q=node/679.

Souder, William. *On a Farther Shore: The Life and Legacy of Rachel Carson*. New York: Crown Publishers, 2012.

Spooner, Alecia M. *Environmental Science for Dummies*. Hoboken, NJ: J. Wiley & Sons, 2012.

Steingraber, Sandra. "The Fracking of Rachel Carson." *Orion* magazine, August 2012. https://orionmagazine.org/article /the-fracking-of-rachel-carson/.

Stone, Michael K., and Zenobia Barlow, eds. *Ecological Literacy: Educating Our Children for a Sustainable World*. San Francisco: Sierra Club Books, 2005.

Swaby, Rachel. "Rachel Carson." In *Headstrong: 52 Women Who Changed Science—and the World*, 75-79. New York: Broadway Books, 2015.

Taylor, A. J. P. *The Origins of the Second World War*. New York: Atheneum, 1962.

"Theo Colborn, 1927-2014." TEDX. Accessed June 17, 2016. http://endocrinedisruption.org/about-tedx/theo-colborn.

Venezia, Mike. *Rachel Carson: Clearing the Way for Environmental Protection*. New York: Children's Press, 2010.

Wadsworth, Ginger. *Rachel Carson, Voice for the Earth*. Minneapolis: Lerner Publications, 1992.

Walker, Bruce. "The Grim 50th Anniversary of *Silent Spring*." *The New American*, September 27, 2012. http://www.thenewamerican.com/culture/history/item/12996-the-grim-50th-anniversary-of-silent-spring.

Wiegand, Steve. *Lessons from the Great Depression for Dummies*. Hoboken, NJ: Wiley Pub., 2009.

Wikipedia Contributors. "History of Ecology." *Wikipedia*. Accessed June 10, 2016. https://en.wikipedia.org/w/index.php?title=History_of_ecology&oldid=721919572.

Wikipedia Contributors. "Marjorie Spock." *Wikipedia*. April 20, 2016. Accessed June 16, 2016. https://en.wikipedia.org/wiki/Marjorie_Spock.

Woodin, Sarah (Sally), Dr. "Interview with Sally Woodin." E-mail interview by author. June 23, 2016.

Worster, Donald. *Nature's Economy: A History of Ecological Ideas.* Second Edition ed. New York: Cambridge University Press, 1994.

Zieger, Robert H. *America's Great War: World War I and the American Experience.* Lanham, MD: Rowman & Littlefield Publishers, 2000.

Zinsser, Judith P. *History & Feminism: A Glass Half Full.* New York: Twayne Publishers, 1993.

INDEX

Page numbers in **boldface** are illustrations. Entries in **boldface** are glossary terms.

Cottam, Clarence, 63–66, 69, 73, 75

Darwin, Charles, 46–47
Davis, Jeanne, 73
DDT. *see* **Chemical** DDT
Department of Fisheries, 22, 32
dichlorodiphenyl-trichloroethane, 5–6, 24

ecology, 6, 43, 45–46, 51, 56
    scientific method of, 51–52
ecosystem, 6, 29, 44, 59, 98
Egler, Frank, 55, 66–69, **68**, 73
endocrine system, 97
endocrine-disrupting
    chemicals, 96–97
Enola Gay, **58**
entomology, 61
environment protection, the
    future of, 7, 66, 106–107
environmental movement,
    89, 98
environmental pollution, 28–29,
    67, 92
**Environmental Protection
    Agency (EPA)**, 85, 92–93
environmental toxicology, 55
environmentalism, 53

finches, 46–47
fire ant, 35, 63, 66
Food and Drug Administration
    (FDA), 28
food chain, 55, 57
food web, 49
fossil fuels, 50

global climate change, 50
Great Depression, 17, 27, 30,
    32–33, 38
Great Lakes, 96–97
gypsy moth, 35, 36–37, **37**, 62

Haney, Bette, 73–74
Hargraves, Malcolm, 74, 75
Hayes, Wayland, 78, 79–80
hematologist, 74
Higgins, Elmer, 32, 63
Hiroshima, 26, 33
hormones, 97

insect eradication programs, 75

Jim Crow laws, 26
Johns Hopkins University, 30

Knipling, Edward, 70–72, **71**

ABOUT THE AUTHOR

Meghan Rock is a scientific writer and illustrator. Her background is in art, writing, and invertebrate biology. For a time she worked and lived as a marine biologist in the Pacific Northwest and, like Rachel Carson, she feels drawn to the sea. Her illustrations have been used in presentations and papers around the world and span the range from invertebrate biology to forensic science. She lives in land-locked Chicago, where she enjoys hiking with her dog, teaching art to young students, going to museums, and reading in the company of her cat.